MW00439590

# Prayers of
# Christian
# Consolation

Other Loyola Press books
by William G. Storey

**A Catholic Book of Hours and Other Devotions**

**The Complete Rosary**
**A Guide to Praying the Mysteries**

**Novenas**
**Prayers of Intercession and Devotion**

**A Prayer Book of Catholic Devotions**
**Praying the Seasons and Feasts of the Church Year**

# Prayers of Christian Consolation

Composed, edited, and translated by
William G. Storey,
Professor Emeritus of Liturgy,
University of Notre Dame

LOYOLA PRESS.
A JESUIT MINISTRY

Chicago

# LOYOLA PRESS.
## A JESUIT MINISTRY

3441 N. Ashland Avenue
Chicago, Illinois 60657
(800) 621-1008
www.loyolapress.com

© 2008 William G. Storey
All rights reserved

*Nihil Obstat*
Reverend William H. Woestman, O.M.I., J.C.D.
Censor Deputatus
April 17, 2008

*Imprimatur*
Reverend John F. Canary, S.T.L., D.Min.
Vicar General
Archdiocese of Chicago
April 21, 2008

The *Nihil Obstat* and *Imprimatur* are official declarations that a book is free of doctrinal and moral error. No implication is contained therein that those who have granted the *Nihil Obstat* and *Imprimatur* agree with the content, opinions, or statements expressed. Nor do they assume any legal responsibility associated with publication.

*Interior design by Donna Antkowiak*

**Library of Congress Cataloging-in-Publication Data**
Prayers of Christian consolation / compiled, edited, and translated by William G. Storey.
    p. cm.
  Includes bibliographical references.
  ISBN-13: 978-0-8294-2585-7
  ISBN-10: 0-8294-2585-3
 1. Consolation. 2. Suffering—Religious aspects—Catholic Church. 3. Catholic Church—Prayers and devotions. I. Storey, William George, 1923–
  BX2373.S5P73 2008
  242'.86—dc22

                                                    2008013182

Printed in China
08 09 10 11 12 13 RRD 10 9 8 7 6 5 4 3 2 1

# Contents

**Introduction**                                                        xvii

# *I*
# *Essential Prayers*

## Foundations of Our Faith                                      1

The Gospel in Brief ........................ 1
The Canticle of the Incarnate Word.......... 1
The Greatest Commandment ............... 3
The New Commandment.................... 3
The Gentle Mastery of Christ............... 4
For God Alone .......................... 5
Faith and Trust in Jesus.................... 6
Prayer of Commitment..................... 6
For God's Help........................... 7
Poem .................................. 7
The Holy Gospel according to Julian
   of Norwich ........................... 8
St. Patrick's Creed ....................... 9

## Basic Christian Prayers                                     10

The Sign of the Cross ..................... 10
The Apostles' Creed: Credo in Deum ........ 10
The Lord's Prayer: Pater Noster............. 12

**v**

The Lesser Doxology: Gloria Patri. . . . . . . . . . . 13
The Greater Doxology: Gloria in
   Excelsis Deo . . . . . . . . . . . . . . . . . . . . . . 13
The Angelical Salutation: Ave, Maria. . . . . . . . 14
The Angelus. . . . . . . . . . . . . . . . . . . . . . . . . 15
The Regina Coeli . . . . . . . . . . . . . . . . . . . . . 16
The Simple Path. . . . . . . . . . . . . . . . . . . . . . 17
The Guiding Light of Eternity . . . . . . . . . . . . . 17
Evening Hymn . . . . . . . . . . . . . . . . . . . . . . . 17
Night Prayer . . . . . . . . . . . . . . . . . . . . . . . . . 18
Prayer before Sleep . . . . . . . . . . . . . . . . . . . 18
Prayer before Sleep . . . . . . . . . . . . . . . . . . . 19
Universal Prayer for Peace . . . . . . . . . . . . . . 20
Prayer for Peacefulness. . . . . . . . . . . . . . . . . 20
Prayer of Abandonment . . . . . . . . . . . . . . . . 20

## Prayers to Jesus                                    22

Jesus Help Me . . . . . . . . . . . . . . . . . . . . . . . 22
Peace Prayer . . . . . . . . . . . . . . . . . . . . . . . . 22
Jesus Needs Us. . . . . . . . . . . . . . . . . . . . . . 23
Hymn to Jesus . . . . . . . . . . . . . . . . . . . . . . . 24
Invocations to Christ Our Lord. . . . . . . . . . . . . 24
The Jesus Prayer . . . . . . . . . . . . . . . . . . . . . 26
The Most Holy Name of Jesus. . . . . . . . . . . . . 26
A Prayer before Holy Communion . . . . . . . . . . 28
To Jesus in Our Tabernacles . . . . . . . . . . . . . 29
For True Devotion to the Blessed Sacrament . . . 30
To Our Most Holy Redeemer. . . . . . . . . . . . . . 31
Prayer to the Son of God . . . . . . . . . . . . . . . . 32

Prayer before the Blessed Sacrament. . . . . . . . . 32

A Visit to the Blessed Sacrament . . . . . . . . . . . 33

Prayer in Full Faith . . . . . . . . . . . . . . . . . . . . . . 34

A Prayer for Deliverance . . . . . . . . . . . . . . . . . 35

A Prayer for Help . . . . . . . . . . . . . . . . . . . . . . . 35

Hymn to the Sacred Heart of Jesus. . . . . . . . . . 36

Cast All Care on God Who Cares for You . . . . . 36

Doxology. . . . . . . . . . . . . . . . . . . . . . . . . . . . . . 37

Steal Away . . . . . . . . . . . . . . . . . . . . . . . . . . . . 37

Poem: Light Shines Out of Darkness. . . . . . . . . 38

Jesus My Friend. . . . . . . . . . . . . . . . . . . . . . . . 39

Hymn . . . . . . . . . . . . . . . . . . . . . . . . . . . . . . . . 39

## Devotions to Christ Crucified     41

Antiphon. . . . . . . . . . . . . . . . . . . . . . . . . . . . . . . 41

The Sufferings of Jesus. . . . . . . . . . . . . . . . . . . 41

The Holy Face of Jesus . . . . . . . . . . . . . . . . . . . 42

Jesus Crucified. . . . . . . . . . . . . . . . . . . . . . . . . 43

Christ Crucified. . . . . . . . . . . . . . . . . . . . . . . . . 44

Five Holy Cross Prayers . . . . . . . . . . . . . . . . . 45

Prayer to Jesus Crucified. . . . . . . . . . . . . . . . . 48

To the Five Wounds of Jesus. . . . . . . . . . . . . . 48

Hail, Sacred Heart of Jesus. . . . . . . . . . . . . . . 57

To the Sacred Heart of Jesus . . . . . . . . . . . . . 58

Litany of the Sacred Passion. . . . . . . . . . . . . . 59

The Mother of Sorrows. . . . . . . . . . . . . . . . . . . 63

Easter Day . . . . . . . . . . . . . . . . . . . . . . . . . . . . 63

## Prayers to the Blessed Virgin Mary 65

The Canticle of Mary . . . . . . . . . . . . . . . . . . . . . . 66
Sub Tuum Praesidium . . . . . . . . . . . . . . . . . . . . . 67
Ave, Maris Stella . . . . . . . . . . . . . . . . . . . . . . . . . 68
Salve, Regina . . . . . . . . . . . . . . . . . . . . . . . . . . . 69
Te Matrem laudamus . . . . . . . . . . . . . . . . . . . . . . 69
Salutation to the Blessed Virgin . . . . . . . . . . . . . 71
Memorare . . . . . . . . . . . . . . . . . . . . . . . . . . . . . . . 72
To Mary . . . . . . . . . . . . . . . . . . . . . . . . . . . . . . . . 73
A Marian Anthem . . . . . . . . . . . . . . . . . . . . . . . . . 73
To Our Lady of Consolation . . . . . . . . . . . . . . . . . 74
Antiphon of St. Francis . . . . . . . . . . . . . . . . . . . . 75
To Mary for the Sick . . . . . . . . . . . . . . . . . . . . . . 76
To Our Sorrowful Mother . . . . . . . . . . . . . . . . . . . 77
To Our Lady of Guadalupe . . . . . . . . . . . . . . . . . . 78
Prayer to Our Lady of Combermere . . . . . . . . . . 79
A Prayer to St. Joseph in Time of Need . . . . . . . 80

# II
# Prayers of Petition and Consolation

## Prayers for the Ill, Infirm, and Dying 81

Prayers for the Sick . . . . . . . . . . . . . . . . . . . . . . . 81
In Time of Sickness . . . . . . . . . . . . . . . . . . . . . . . 82
For Acceptance in Suffering . . . . . . . . . . . . . . . . 82

For Healing. . . . . . . . . . . . . . . . . . . . . . . . . . . . . . . .83

In Old Age . . . . . . . . . . . . . . . . . . . . . . . . . . . . . . .84

For the Redemptive Use of Suffering . . . . . . . .85

Thanksgiving for Recovery . . . . . . . . . . . . . . . . .86

At the Hour of Death . . . . . . . . . . . . . . . . . . . . .87

A Prayer for the Dying . . . . . . . . . . . . . . . . . . . .88

Prayer of St. Macrina on Her Deathbed . . . . . . .88

For the Dying . . . . . . . . . . . . . . . . . . . . . . . . . . . .89

For Those We Love . . . . . . . . . . . . . . . . . . . . . . .90

Passing Over . . . . . . . . . . . . . . . . . . . . . . . . . . . .90

For Momma, in a Coma at the Hour
   of Death . . . . . . . . . . . . . . . . . . . . . . . . . . . . . .91

In Paradisum . . . . . . . . . . . . . . . . . . . . . . . . . . . .92

Subvenite . . . . . . . . . . . . . . . . . . . . . . . . . . . . . . .92

For the Dying . . . . . . . . . . . . . . . . . . . . . . . . . . . .93

Abide with Me. . . . . . . . . . . . . . . . . . . . . . . . . . . .93

Good Friday . . . . . . . . . . . . . . . . . . . . . . . . . . . . .94

The Cross. . . . . . . . . . . . . . . . . . . . . . . . . . . . . . .95

Peace at the Last . . . . . . . . . . . . . . . . . . . . . . . . .95

## Prayers for the Dead 96

A Living Hope. . . . . . . . . . . . . . . . . . . . . . . . . . . .96

For the Faithful Departed. . . . . . . . . . . . . . . . . . .96

Dies Irae. . . . . . . . . . . . . . . . . . . . . . . . . . . . . . . .98

Psalm 130: De Profundis . . . . . . . . . . . . . . . . . . .99

O Christ, You Wept. . . . . . . . . . . . . . . . . . . . . . . 100

For Our Dear Departed . . . . . . . . . . . . . . . . . . . 101

Prayer for a Stillborn Child. . . . . . . . . . . . . . . . . 102

Prayer for a Dead Child . . . . . . . . . . . . . . . . . . . 102

For Those Who Survive . . . . . . . . . . . . . . . . . . . 103
Litany of the Faithful Departed. . . . . . . . . . . . . 103

## Prayers in Times of Distress 107

Prayer in Despair . . . . . . . . . . . . . . . . . . . . . . . 107
Psalm 13. . . . . . . . . . . . . . . . . . . . . . . . . . . . . . 107
Help Me to Remember. . . . . . . . . . . . . . . . . . . . 108
In the Time of Distress. . . . . . . . . . . . . . . . . . . . 109
In Desolation . . . . . . . . . . . . . . . . . . . . . . . . . . 109
In Time of Temptation . . . . . . . . . . . . . . . . . . . 110
In Time of Anxiety . . . . . . . . . . . . . . . . . . . . . . 112
For the Unemployed. . . . . . . . . . . . . . . . . . . . . 113
For the Frustrated. . . . . . . . . . . . . . . . . . . . . . . 114
For the Mentally Afflicted . . . . . . . . . . . . . . . . . 115
Prayer of Submission. . . . . . . . . . . . . . . . . . . . 115
Laid Off. . . . . . . . . . . . . . . . . . . . . . . . . . . . . . . 116
For the Parents of Teenagers . . . . . . . . . . . . . 117
For a Troubled Family . . . . . . . . . . . . . . . . . . . 118
In Time of Divorce . . . . . . . . . . . . . . . . . . . . . . 119
In Widowhood. . . . . . . . . . . . . . . . . . . . . . . . . . 120
Against Addiction . . . . . . . . . . . . . . . . . . . . . . . 122
A Final Prayer. . . . . . . . . . . . . . . . . . . . . . . . . . 123

## Prayers of Petition 124

Christ in Us. . . . . . . . . . . . . . . . . . . . . . . . . . . . 124
For Blessed Unity. . . . . . . . . . . . . . . . . . . . . . . 124
For a Good Marriage . . . . . . . . . . . . . . . . . . . . 125
For the Blessings of Home . . . . . . . . . . . . . . . 125
For Peace and Quiet . . . . . . . . . . . . . . . . . . . . 126

For Spouses. . . . . . . . . . . . . . . . . . . . . . . . . . . . 127
For Our Parish . . . . . . . . . . . . . . . . . . . . . . . . 128
For Trust and Humility . . . . . . . . . . . . . . . . . . 130
For Holiness. . . . . . . . . . . . . . . . . . . . . . . . . . . 131
For Perfect Love. . . . . . . . . . . . . . . . . . . . . . . . 131
For Patience. . . . . . . . . . . . . . . . . . . . . . . . . . . 132
For Fresh Courage. . . . . . . . . . . . . . . . . . . . . . 133
For Perfect Confidence . . . . . . . . . . . . . . . . . . 134
For the Fullness of Our Baptism . . . . . . . . . . . 135
For the Gift of Wisdom. . . . . . . . . . . . . . . . . . . 136
For Divine Correction. . . . . . . . . . . . . . . . . . . . 138
For Christian Friendship. . . . . . . . . . . . . . . . . . 138
For Divine Wisdom. . . . . . . . . . . . . . . . . . . . . . 139
For Reverence in Prayer . . . . . . . . . . . . . . . . . 140

## For Repentance and Forgiveness   142

Noverim Me, Noverim Te . . . . . . . . . . . . . . . . . 142
For the Gift of Repentance . . . . . . . . . . . . . . . 143
For Repentance and Forgiveness . . . . . . . . . . 144
Prayer to Be Forgiven . . . . . . . . . . . . . . . . . . . 145
The Trisagion of Sanctification. . . . . . . . . . . . . 145
Christ in the Universe. . . . . . . . . . . . . . . . . . . . 146
To Christ Crucified . . . . . . . . . . . . . . . . . . . . . . 147
The Seven Deadly Sins and Their Remedies . . 148
How Virtue Drives Out Vice. . . . . . . . . . . . . . . 151
Invocation. . . . . . . . . . . . . . . . . . . . . . . . . . . . . 152
Who Is There to Understand? . . . . . . . . . . . . . 152
To Know My Sins . . . . . . . . . . . . . . . . . . . . . . . 153
For the Forgiveness of Sins. . . . . . . . . . . . . . . 153

# III
# Prayers of Gratitude and Thanksgiving

## Hymns of Praise     156

Thank You Jesus!. . . . . . . . . . . . . . . . . . . . . . . . 156
Prayer of Thanksgiving. . . . . . . . . . . . . . . . . . 157
A General Prayer of Thanksgiving. . . . . . . . . . 158
Litany of Praise and Thanksgiving. . . . . . . . . . 158
Holy Father of Glory. . . . . . . . . . . . . . . . . . . . . 160
Invocation. . . . . . . . . . . . . . . . . . . . . . . . . . . . . 160
For the Holy Women of Israel . . . . . . . . . . . . . 161
Hymn of Praise. . . . . . . . . . . . . . . . . . . . . . . . . 161
The Divine Praises. . . . . . . . . . . . . . . . . . . . . . 162
Hymn to the Holy Spirit . . . . . . . . . . . . . . . . . . 163
A Morning Prayer to the Holy Spirit . . . . . . . . . 165
A Prayer for Help . . . . . . . . . . . . . . . . . . . . . . . 166

## Praise from Scripture and the Saints  167

To Jesus. . . . . . . . . . . . . . . . . . . . . . . . . . . . . . 167
The Canticle of the Church . . . . . . . . . . . . . . . 167
The Canticle of All Creatures. . . . . . . . . . . . . . 169
Psalm 117: Act of Praise . . . . . . . . . . . . . . . . 171
The Praises of God after Francis
    Received the Stigmata . . . . . . . . . . . . . . . . . 172

Canticle of Moses. . . . . . . . . . . . . . . . . . . . . . . . 174
A Canticle of King David . . . . . . . . . . . . . . . . . 175
Canticle of Tobit . . . . . . . . . . . . . . . . . . . . . . . . 176
A Canticle of Judith . . . . . . . . . . . . . . . . . . . . . 177
The Righteous in the Sight of God . . . . . . . . . . 178
A Prayer for Wisdom . . . . . . . . . . . . . . . . . . . . 179
Prayer of Wise Solomon . . . . . . . . . . . . . . . . . 180
Our Messiah and Lord . . . . . . . . . . . . . . . . . . . 180
God Is My Salvation. . . . . . . . . . . . . . . . . . . . . 181
The Prince of Peace. . . . . . . . . . . . . . . . . . . . . 182
Our Incomparable God . . . . . . . . . . . . . . . . . . 183
God's Servant. . . . . . . . . . . . . . . . . . . . . . . . . . 184
God's Promise . . . . . . . . . . . . . . . . . . . . . . . . . 185
The Great Transit . . . . . . . . . . . . . . . . . . . . . . . 186

# IV

# Invocations, Litanies, and Prayers in Special Seasons

## Prayers in Special Seasons

Prayer in Advent. . . . . . . . . . . . . . . . . . . . . . . . 187
Prayer in Christmastide . . . . . . . . . . . . . . . . . . 188

Prayer in Lent. . . . . . . . . . . . . . . . . . . . . . . . . . . 190
Hymn of St. Patrick . . . . . . . . . . . . . . . . . . . . . 190
Prayer in Holy Week. . . . . . . . . . . . . . . . . . . . . 191
Prayer in Eastertide . . . . . . . . . . . . . . . . . . . . 193
The Coronation Hymn . . . . . . . . . . . . . . . . . . . 193

## Special Invocations 195

To the Blessed Trinity. . . . . . . . . . . . . . . . . . . . 195
To the Holy Spirit . . . . . . . . . . . . . . . . . . . . . . . 196
Prayer to the Holy Spirit. . . . . . . . . . . . . . . . . . 197
To the Sacred Heart of Jesus . . . . . . . . . . . . . 197
Prayer before a Crucifix . . . . . . . . . . . . . . . . . . 198
The Precious Blood of Jesus. . . . . . . . . . . . . . 198
In Honor of the Holy Cross . . . . . . . . . . . . . . . 199
To St. John the Baptist, Jesus' Forerunner . . . . 199
To Michael the Archangel, Prince of the
   Heavenly Host . . . . . . . . . . . . . . . . . . . . . . . 200
To St. Joseph, Patron of the Dying . . . . . . . . . 201
To Padre Pio of Pietralcina. . . . . . . . . . . . . . . . 202
To Mother Teresa of Calcutta. . . . . . . . . . . . . . 202
To Dorothy Day. . . . . . . . . . . . . . . . . . . . . . . . . 203

## Litanies of Intercession 205

Litany of the Holy Name of Jesus . . . . . . . . . . 205
Litany of the Sacred Heart of Jesus . . . . . . . . 208
Litany of the Resurrection . . . . . . . . . . . . . . . . 210
Litany of the Blessed Sacrament. . . . . . . . . . . 212
Litany of Loreto. . . . . . . . . . . . . . . . . . . . . . . . . 214
Litany of St. Joseph . . . . . . . . . . . . . . . . . . . . 216

Litany of the Seven Gifts of the Spirit . . . . . . . . 218
Litany of the Beatitudes . . . . . . . . . . . . . . . . . . 219

# V

# Sacraments

## A Preparation for Holy Communion in the Home
226

## A Preparation for the Sacrament of Anointing
231

Notes . . . . . . . . . . . . . . . . . . . . . . . . . . . . . . . 235
Acknowledgments . . . . . . . . . . . . . . . . . . . . . . 242
About the Author . . . . . . . . . . . . . . . . . . . . . . . 246

# *Introduction*

This collection of prayers is intended for those who are seeking consolation in a time of suffering. Those who use this book will discover the Lord's remedies for sickness, pain, loss, grief, depression, moral confusion, sickness of soul, and other troubles that befall us in this vale of tears. As we lift our hearts in prayer to our loving Father in heaven, God will reveal to us the true meaning of suffering and alleviate our pain and bewilderment. Jesus is the preacher of good news—especially to those who need it most.

Prayer has two aspects: one human; one divine.

The *human* aspect reflects the effort to lift one's mind and heart to God (*sursum corda*) by saying the inspired texts of our religion: the psalms and basic prayers of our faith; favorite passages from the Holy Scriptures; and the spiritual writings of saints, poets, mystics, theologians, and other sincere Christians.

The *divine* aspect is the Holy Spirit poured into our hearts at our baptism. The abiding spirit of God is *prayer itself* at the center of our being. This prayer is the divine, personal, inner energy that cries out to God and for God at every beat of our existence. This divine presence urges us toward God and inspires us to express our spiritual selves in prayer, whether we want to or not. Our part in this push of divine energy is to wait, to listen, to meditate, to long for God with all our hearts.

This book is a collection of prayers to be prayed by Christians in distress. It draws from our Catholic tradition. We Catholics are members of a great, world-wide community of prayer that has developed over thousands of years. We are privileged to draw upon that tradition here.

This collection includes many forms of prayer: psalms and canticles from the Old Testament, hymns from the New Testament and from later Christian history, other passages from the Bible, Christian poetry of many eras, prose texts from different centuries to stimulate devotion, and many prayers from saints and mystics and other Christians.

Our Catholic faith is not primarily designed to ease us over life's difficulties or to comfort us superficially. Rather, it is a profound view of reality as God has revealed it to us in Christ. It is a deep view of things. It provides us with a formation in faith that changes our natural way of seeing and behaving so that we find ourselves conformed to the Christ-life as it is revealed in the Holy Gospels.

By holy baptism we become new persons in a radical way and are prepared for the life of faith—prepared to engage in a lifelong struggle to conform ourselves to Christ our Lord. He is our life model. We are called to walk in his footsteps, to love our fellow humans, to embrace the cross, and to grow in holiness through the sacraments and personal and persistent prayer until we obtain the mind of Christ.

Following this model means that when we are troubled, tested, and tempted, we must try to avoid the natural complaining, bewailing, and griping to which we are prone and turn ourselves over to Jesus, our precious Lord and teacher.

Above all, for our consolation, we must ground ourselves on the bedrock of the faith and remember the following three points:

1. *God is love and loves each one of us individually. Every hair of our head is counted and* not even a sparrow falls from heaven without our Father's knowledge (Matthew 10:29–31). By divine decree, our destiny is heaven and "all the way to heaven is heaven, for Jesus said, 'I am the way'" (St. Catherine of Siena).

2. *God in Christ is ever present to us and for us.* God is not absent or distant but infinitely present in our lives. Not only can't we escape the presence of God but we are immersed in it in time and for eternity. Jesus is our intimate friend and cares for us at every moment of our existence.

3. *The royal road of the cross is the certified way to heaven.* Jesus traveled it himself and calls us to do the same in our own way and place:

   *Jesus summoned the crowd with his disciples and said to them, "Whoever wishes to come after me must deny himself, take up his cross, and follow me. For whoever wishes to save his life will lose it, but whoever loses his life for my sake and that of the gospel will save it. What profit is there for one to gain the whole world and forfeit his life? What could one give in exchange for his life?" (Mark 8:34–37, NAB).*

   Consider this praise of the cross from *The Imitation of Christ,* by Thomas à Kempis:

   *In the Cross is health, in the Cross is life, in the Cross is protection from enemies, in the Cross is fullness of heavenly sweetness, in the Cross is strength of mind, joy of spirit, height of virtue, full perfection of all holiness, and there is no help for the soul, or hope of everlasting life, save through the virtue of the Cross.*

*Take, therefore, your cross and follow Jesus, and you shall go to life everlasting. He has gone before you, bearing His Cross, and died for you upon that Cross so that you should in like manner bear with Him the Cross of penance and tribulation, and that you should be ready in like manner for His love to suffer death, if need be, as He has done for you. If you die with Him you will live with Him; if you are His companion in pain, you will be His companion in glory.*[1]

May you find consolation here. This book is dedicated to the blood of Jesus shed on the cross for us and to the tears of our Lady of Consolation who stood by him as he suffered and died.

*Blessed be the God and Father of our Lord Jesus Christ, the Father of mercies and the God of all consolation, who consoles us in all our affliction, so that we may be able to console those who are in any affliction with the consolation with which we ourselves are consoled by God. For just as the sufferings of Christ are abundant for us, so also our consolation is abundant through Christ.*

2 Corinthians 1:3-5

# I
# *Essential Prayers*

## Foundations of Our Faith

### *The Gospel in Brief*
God so loved the world that he gave his only Son,
so that everyone who believes in him
might not perish but might have eternal life.

John 3:16, NAB

### *The Canticle of the Incarnate Word*
This prologue to John's Gospel derives from a very
early Christian hymn that speaks of the preexistent
Word of God who assumed our humanity and enables
us to become the children of God. This sublime pas-
sage of Scripture is the foundation of our belief in the
Incarnation, for us and for our salvation. This life-giving
doctrine is the root of our hope, replacing our fears with
joy and gratitude!

In the beginning was the Word,
and the Word was with God,
and the Word was God.
He was in the beginning with God.
All things came to be through him,

and without him nothing came to be.
What came to be through him was life,
and this life was the light of the human race;
the light shines in the darkness,
and the darkness has not overcome it.

He was in the world,
and the world came to be through him,
but the world did not know him.
He came to what was his own,
but his own people did not accept him.

But to those who did accept him,
he gave power to become children of God,
to those who believe in his name,
who were born not by natural generation
nor by human choice nor by a man's decision
but of God.

And the Word became flesh
and made his dwelling among us,
and we saw his glory,
the glory as of the Father's only Son,
full of grace and truth.

John 1:1–5, 10–14, NAB

**PRAYER**
Eternal Word of God,
become flesh for our sake,
we accept you and thank you
for what we all receive from you.

By your gracious gift, we have every right
to complete confidence in your love for us
and, by believing in your name,
have the power to become your very children,
partaking of your divine nature.
Blest are you, O Savior of the world,
now and for ever.
~AMEN.

## *The Greatest Commandment*

One of the scribes asked Jesus,
"Which is the first of all the commandments?"
Jesus replied, "The first is this:
'Hear, O Israel! The Lord our God is the Lord
    alone!
You shall love the Lord your God with all your
    heart,
with all your soul, with all your mind, and with
    all your strength.'
The second is this: 'You shall love your neighbor
    as yourself.'
There is no other commandment greater than
    these."

Mark 12:28–31, NAB

## *The New Commandment*

At the Last Supper Jesus said to his disciples,
"I give you a new commandment:
Love one another.
As I have loved you,

so you also should love one another.
This is how all will know that you are my
    disciples,
if you have love for one another."

John 13:34–35, NAB

God is love, and those who abide in love abide in
God, and God abides in them.

1 John 4:16

###### PRAYER

Lord Jesus, Teacher of Righteousness,
you complete even the great commandments
by giving us the new commandment of love.
Help us to dedicate ourselves to loving and
serving the Body of Christ in this world
in order to find perfect bliss in the next.
You live and reign for ever and ever.
Amen.

### *The Gentle Mastery of Christ*

Come to me,
all you who labor and are burdened,
and I will give you rest.
Take my yoke upon you and learn from me,
for I am meek and humble of heart
and you will find rest for yourselves.
For my yoke is easy,
and my burden light.

Matthew 11:28–30, NAB

Father,
we rejoice in the gifts of love
we have received from the heart of Jesus your Son.
Open our hearts to share his life
and continue to bless us with his love.
We ask this through Christ our Lord.
Amen.[2]


## *For God Alone*

Almighty, eternal, just and merciful God,
grant us in our misery that we may do for you
    alone
what we know you want us to do
and always want what pleases you;
so that cleansed and enlightened interiorly,
and fired with the ardor of the Holy Spirit,
we may be able to follow
in the footprints of your Son, our Lord Jesus
    Christ,
and so make our way to you,
by your grace alone, Most High,
who live and reign in perfect Trinity and simple
    Unity,
and are glorified, God all-powerful,
for ever and ever. Amen

St. Francis of Assisi (1181–1226)[3]

### Faith and Trust in Jesus

Lord Jesus Christ,
on the human side you are sprung from David's
      line,
God's Son according to God's will and power,
truly born of the Virgin Mary,
baptized by John to fulfill all righteousness,
and actually crucified for us in the flesh
under Pontius Pilate and Herod the Tetrarch.
On the third day you raised a banner
to rally your saints and believers in every age,
united in the single body of your Church.
By the grace and power of these mysteries,
fit us out with unshakable faith,
nail us body and soul to your cross,
and establish us in love by the blood you shed for
      us,
O Savior of the world,
whose reign is a reign for all ages.
~AMEN.[4]

### Prayer of Commitment

Lord Jesus, our Messiah,
the reflection of God's glory
and the exact imprint of God's very being:
We entrust our lives to you
by renewing the promises of our baptism,
our commitment to our church community,

and our desire to do your holy will,
now and always, and for ever and ever.
~Amen.

### For God's Help

Lord my God,
rescue me from myself,
and give me to you;
take away from me everything
that draws me from you,
and give me all those things
that lead me to you;
for Jesus Christ's sake.
~Amen.

Abbot Louis de Blois (1506–1566)

### Poem

Prayer, the Church's banquet, Angel's age,
God's breath in man returning to his birth,
The soul in paraphrase, heart in pilgrimage,
The Christian plummet, sounding heaven and
      earth;
Engine against the Almighty, sinner's tower,
Reversed thunder, Christ-side-piercing spear,
The six-days' world transposing in an hour,
A kind of tune, which all things hear and fear;
Softness, and peace, and joy, and love, and bliss,
Exalted manna, gladness of the best,
Heaven in ordinary, man well drest,

The milky way, the bird of Paradise,
Church-bells beyond the stars heard, the soul's
    blood,
The land of spices; something understood.

George Herbert (1593–1633)

## The Holy Gospel according to Julian of Norwich

Puzzled and confused by the sight of sin, its causes and its effects, the mystic Julian of Norwich (1343–ca. 1423) received strong assurance from our Lord that "all will be well, and every kind of thing will be well." This assurance was intended not only for her personally but for all her fellow Christians who struggle to understand the dilemma raised both by sin itself and by the promise that God will completely overcome it.

And so our good Lord answered to all the questions and doubts which I could raise, saying most comfortingly in this fashion: I will make all things well, I shall make all things well, I may make all things well, and I can make all things well; and you will see that yourself, that all things will be well. . . . And in these five words God wishes to be enclosed in rest and in peace. . . . I understand powerful consolation from all the deeds of our Lord which are still to be performed; for just as the blessed Trinity created everything from nothing, just so the same blessed Trinity will make well all things which are not well. It is God's will that we pay great heed to all the deeds which he has performed, for he wishes us to know from them all which he will do; and he revealed that to me by those words which he said: "And you will see yourself that every kind of thing will be well."[5]

## *St. Patrick's Creed*

Our God, God of all humanity,
God of heaven and earth, of seas and rivers,
God of sun and moon and all the stars,
God of the high mountains and the lowly valleys,
God above heaven and in heaven and under
     heaven.
God dwells in heaven and earth and sea
and in everything that is in them.

God inspires all things,
gives life to everything,
is above all things,
and supports everything.

God makes the sun shine,
gives light for the moon,
creates springs in the desert,
sets islands in the seas,
and provides stars for the galaxies.

God has a coeternal and consubstantial Son;
the Son is not younger than the Father,
the Father is not older than the Son.

The Holy Spirit breathes in them both;
the Father, the Son, and the Holy Spirit
are undivided.[6]

# Basic Christian Prayers

These foundational prayers contain all that is most needful for a Christian. Please memorize them and say them each day with great care, reverence, and personal commitment. For guidance, remember these words of Mother Teresa of Calcutta (1910–1997):

> *Start and end the day with prayer. Come to God as a child. If you find it hard to pray you can say, "Come, Holy Spirit, guide me, protect me, clear out my mind so that I can pray." Or, if you pray to Mary, you can say, "Mary, Mother of Jesus, be a mother to me now, help me to pray."*[7]

## The Sign of the Cross

> Invest and guard each of your members with this victorious sign, and nothing will harm you.
>
> St. Ephrem of Syria (ca. 306–373)

We begin nearly all liturgical worship and our personal prayers with this invocation and profession of faith. The sign itself—forehead to chest, left shoulder to right—signifies Jesus' passion and death; the words that accompany it assert our belief and trust in the Holy Trinity.

In the name of the Father, † and of the Son, and of the Holy Spirit. Amen.

## The Apostles' Creed: Credo in Deum

The Apostles' Creed is a statement of our belief, but it is also a prayer that situates this belief within our spirit of commitment to the Blessed Trinity. It says three times, "I believe *in* . . ." Believing *in* is a lot more than believing *that* . . . Believing *in* is an act of surrender to the Father, the Son, and the Holy Spirit; indeed, it is really an act of faith, hope, and love. Its origin lies in the baptismal practice of the Church of Rome, wherein converts were immersed three times in the baptismal pool as they confessed the three persons of the Holy Trinity. Early on, too, it became a part of liturgical and daily private prayer; a kind of renewal of one's baptismal vows each day.

I believe in God the Father almighty,
    creator of heaven and earth.

I believe in Jesus Christ, God's only Son, our Lord,
    who was conceived by the Holy Spirit,
    born of the Virgin Mary,
    suffered under Pontius Pilate,
    was crucified, died, and was buried;
    he descended to the dead.
    On the third day he rose again;
    he ascended into heaven,
    he is seated at the right hand of the Father,
    and he will come to judge the living and the
        dead.

I believe in the Holy Spirit,
    the holy catholic Church,
    the communion of saints,
    the forgiveness of sins,
    the resurrection of the body,
    and the life everlasting. Amen.

### The Lord's Prayer: Pater Noster

Jesus not only addressed God as *Abba*, ("Dearest Father" in Aramaic) but also authorized us to address God in this way. The Gospels of Luke and Matthew give us the best picture of Jesus at prayer and teaching this prayer to his disciples (Luke 11:2–4; Matthew 6:9–13). It is not only a prayer but a model of praying that contains all the basic themes of Christian prayer. According to many Greek manuscripts of the New Testament and the famous *Didache (Teaching of the Twelve Apostles*, ca. 90 A.D.), this prayer, already in the first century, had the familiar conclusion called the doxology: "For the kingdom and the power and the glory are yours, now and for ever. Amen."

> I bow my knees before the Father, from whom every
> family in heaven and on earth takes its name.
>
> Ephesians 3:14 ˒

Our Father in heaven,
   hallowed be your name,
   your kingdom come,
   your will be done,
   on earth as in heaven.
Give us today our daily bread.
Forgive us our sins
   as we forgive those who sin against us.
Save us from the time of trial
   and deliver us from evil.
For the kingdom, the power, and the glory are
      yours
   now and for ever. Amen.

### *The Lesser Doxology: Gloria Patri*
This act of praise (doxology) in honor of the Holy Trinity is used frequently in the Liturgy of the Hours, the Rosary, and in other forms of private prayer.

Glory to the Father, and to the Son, and to the
    Holy Spirit:
as it was in the beginning, is now, and will be for
    ever. Amen.

Or this form:

Praise God, the Abba bearing love;
Praise God, the Servant from above;
Praise God, the Paraclete we share:
O triune God, receive our prayer.[8]

### *The Greater Doxology:*
### *Gloria in Excelsis Deo*
This is an ancient form of praise to the Holy Trinity that is used frequently at Mass in the Roman rite and at Morning Prayer in the Byzantine rite.

Glory to God in the highest,
and peace to God's people on earth.

Lord God, heavenly King,
almighty God and Father,
    we worship you, we give you thanks,
    we praise you for your glory.

Lord Jesus Christ, only Son of the Father,
Lord God, Lamb of God,

you take away the sin of the world:

    have mercy on us;

you are seated at the right hand of the Father:

    receive our prayer.

For you alone are the Holy One,
you alone are the Lord,
you alone are the Most High.

    Jesus Christ,

    with the Holy Spirit,

    in the glory of God the Father. Amen.

### *The Angelical Salutation: Ave, Maria*

The Hail Mary is composed of two quotations from the first chapter of Luke's Gospel (1:28 and 1:42) and an add-on from sixteenth-century usage. It is both a Mariological and Christological form of prayer that declares the blessed state of both Mary and Jesus in the mystery of the Word made flesh and living among us. The holy names of Jesus and Mary were added to the biblical text in the high Middle Ages and became the focal point of devotion.

The Hail Mary is a major component of the most popular of Marian devotions, the holy Rosary, which proposes its recitation two hundred times in the course of meditating on the twenty mysteries. It is also used three times a day during the recitation of the Angelus.

Hail, Mary, full of grace. The Lord is with you.
Blessed are you among women,
and blessed is the fruit of your womb, Jesus.
Holy Mary, mother of God, pray for us sinners,

    now and at the hour of our death. Amen.

### The Angelus

The Franciscans created this daily devotion in the thirteenth century to commemorate the incarnation of Christ with the cooperation of Mary, his mother and ours. Most Catholic parishes ring for it three times a day, at 6 a.m., noon, and 6 p.m.

The angel of the Lord brought the good news to
> Mary,

~AND SHE CONCEIVED BY THE HOLY SPIRIT.

Hail, Mary, full of grace, the Lord is with you.
Blessed are you among women,
and blessed is the fruit of your womb, Jesus.

~HOLY MARY, MOTHER OF GOD, PRAY FOR US
> SINNERS,

NOW AND AT THE HOUR OF OUR DEATH. AMEN.

I am the Lord's servant;

~LET IT HAPPEN AS THE LORD WILLS.

Hail, Mary, full of grace, . . .

The Word was made flesh,

~AND DWELT AMONG US.

Hail, Mary, full of grace, . . .

Pray for us, holy mother of God,

~THAT WE MAY BECOME WORTHY OF THE
> PROMISES OF CHRIST.

Let us pray:

Pour forth, O Lord, your grace into our hearts,

that we, to whom the incarnation of Christ your
     Son
was made known by the message of an angel,
may by his passion and cross
be brought to the glory of his resurrection;
we ask this through the same Christ our Lord.
~AMEN.

## *The Regina Coeli*
In place of the Angelus, we pray this anthem three
times a day during the fifty days of Easter.

Rejoice, O Queen of heaven, alleluia!
FOR THE SON YOU BORE, ALLELUIA!
HAS ARISEN AS HE PROMISED, ALLELUIA!
PRAY FOR US TO GOD THE FATHER, ALLELUIA!

Rejoice O Virgin Mary, alleluia!
~FOR THE LORD HAS REALLY RISEN, ALLELUIA!

Let us pray:
Gracious God,
you brought joy into the world
through the resurrection of your dear Son,
our Lord Jesus Christ.
Through the prayers of his mother, the Virgin
     Mary,
may we obtain the joys of everlasting life.
We ask this through Christ our Lord.
~AMEN.

### The Simple Path

The fruit of silence is
PRAYER.
The fruit of prayer is
FAITH.
The fruit of faith is
LOVE.
The fruit of love is
SERVICE.
The fruit of service is
PEACE.

Mother Teresa of Calcutta (1910–1997) 9

### The Guiding Light of Eternity

O God, who brought us from the rest of last night
To the joyous light of this day,
Bring me from the new light of this day
To the guiding light of eternity.
Oh! from the new light of this day
To the guarding light of eternity.

Alexander Carmichael 10

### Evening Hymn

O radiant Light, O Sun divine,
Of God the Father's deathless face,
O Image of the light sublime
That fills the heavenly dwelling place:

O Son of God, the source of life,
Praise is your due by night and day.

Our happy lips must raise the strain
Of your esteemed and splendid name.

Lord Jesus Christ, as daylight fades,
As shine the lights of eventide,
We praise the Father with the Son,
The Spirit blest, and with them one.[11]

### Night Prayer
Watch, dear Lord,
with those who wake or watch,
or weep tonight,
and give your angels charge
over those who sleep.
Tend your sick ones, Lord Christ,
Rest your weary ones.
Bless your dying ones.
Soothe your suffering ones.
Pity your afflicted ones.
And all for your love's sake.
Amen.

*The Book of Common Prayer*[12]

### Prayer before Sleep
O God, before I sleep,
I remember before you all the people I love,
and now in silence I say their names to you. . . .
All the people who are sad and lonely, old and
    forgotten,
poor and hungry and cold,

in pain of body and distress of mind.
Bless all who specially need your blessing,
and bless me too,
and make this a good night for me.
This I ask for your love's sake.
Amen.

William Barclay (1907–1978)[13]

### Prayer before Sleep
Sleep is an image of death and of the repose of the saints. We set our hearts on God and our guardian angels who stand watch over us by night and by day.

O Jesus without sin,
King of the poor,
You were sorely subdued
Under ban of the wicked,
Shield me this night
    From Judas.

My soul on your arm, O Christ,
You are the King of the City of Heaven,
You it was who bought my soul, O Jesus,
    You it was who sacrificed your life for me.

Protect me because of my sorrow,
For the sake of your passion, your wounds,
    and your blood,
And take me in safety this night
    Near to the City of God.[14]

### Universal Prayer for Peace

Mother Teresa asked that all people of good will pray this at noon every day.

Lead me from death to life,
from falsehood to truth.
Lead me from despair to hope,
from fear to trust.
Lead me from hate to love,
from war to peace.
Let peace fill my heart, my world, my universe.
Amen.

Mother Teresa of Calcutta (1910–1997)

### Prayer for Peacefulness

Let nothing disturb you
Let nothing frighten you
Everything is changing
God alone is changeless
Patience attains the goal
One who has God lacks nothing
God alone fills our needs.

Teresa of Ávila (1515–1582)[15]

### Prayer of Abandonment

Father,
I abandon myself into your hands;
do with me what you will.
Whatever you may do, I thank you:
I am ready for all, I accept all.

Let only your will be done in me,
and in all your creatures—
I wish no more than this, O Lord.
Into your hands I commend my spirit;
I offer it to you with all the love of my heart,
for I love you, Lord, and so need to give myself,
to surrender myself into your hands without
　　　reserve,
and with boundless confidence,
for you are my Father.

Charles de Foucauld (1858–1916)

# Prayers To Jesus

### *Jesus Help Me*

Jesus, help me, your servant,
whom you redeemed by your precious blood:

In every need let me come to you with humble
    trust, saying,
~JESUS, HELP ME.
In all my doubts, perplexities, and temptations,
~JESUS, HELP ME.
In hours of loneliness, weariness, and trial,
~JESUS, HELP ME.
In the failure of my plans and hopes,
~JESUS, HELP ME.
In disappointments, troubles, and sorrows,
~JESUS, HELP ME.
When I throw myself on your tender love
   as Father and Savior,
~JESUS, HELP ME.
When I feel impatient and my cross is heavy,
~JESUS, HELP ME.
When I am ill and my head and hands cannot do
    their work,
~JESUS, HELP ME.
Always, always, in joys or sorrows, in falls
   and shortcomings,
~JESUS, HELP ME.[16]

### *Peace Prayer*

Lord, make me a instrument of your peace:

where there is hatred, let me sow love;
where there is injury, pardon;
where there is doubt, faith;
where there is despair, hope;
where there is darkness, light;
and where there is sadness, joy.
O divine Master,
grant that I may not so much seek
to be consoled as to console,
to be understood as to understand,
to be loved as to love.
For it is in giving that we receive,
it is in pardoning that we are pardoned,
and it is in dying that we are born anew to
eternal life.

Attributed to St. Francis of Assisi (1181–1226)[17]

## Jesus Needs Us

The risen Christ is with us today,
and he continues to need each one of you.
Jesus needs your eyes to continue to see.
He needs your strength to continue to work.
He needs your voice to continue to teach.
He needs your hands to continue to bless.
He needs your heart to continue to love.
And Jesus needs your whole being
to continue to build up his Body, the church.
As we believe, so let us live!

Cardinal Joseph Bernardin (1928–1996)

### Hymn to Jesus

O Jesus, joy of loving hearts,
The fount of life and our true light,
We seek the peace your love imparts
And stand rejoicing in your sight.

Your truth unchanged has ever stood;
You save all those who heed your call;
To those who seek you, you are good,
To those who find you, all in all.

We taste you, Lord, our living bread,
And long to feast upon you still;
We drink of you, the fountainhead,
Our thirsting souls to quench and fill.

For you our restless spirit yearns,
Where'er our changing lot is cast;
Glad, when your presence we discern,
Blest when our faith can hold you fast.

O Jesus, with us ever stay;
Make all our moments calm and bright;
Oh, chase the night of sin away,
Shed o'er the world your holy light.

St. Bernard of Clairvaux (1090–1153)[18]

### Invocations to Christ Our Lord

Lord Christ, Son of the living God,
you humbled yourself by becoming like us
    that we might become like you.

You lodged in the womb of the Virgin Mary
  for us and for our salvation.
You were born in the cave of Bethlehem
  to teach us humility and love of poverty.
You were adored by shepherds and wise men
  and taught us to worship you in our hearts.
You were presented in the temple
  to teach us to surrender ourselves to you.

You were baptized by John in the Jordan
  and created the sacrament of our rebirth.
You spent your life proclaiming the Good News
  and filled our hearts with joy.
You went about doing good in Galilee and Judea,
  driving out demons, healing the sick,
  and raising the dead.

You submitted to suffering and death for our sake
  to save us from all sin and danger.
You died on the cross of bitter pain
  to set us free from sin and death.
You were buried in noble Joseph's tomb
  to give us confidence and hope.

You rose again on the third day
  to fill us with new life and full joy.
You ascended into heaven
  to raise our hearts on high.
You are seated at the right hand of the Father
  to intercede for us, now and for ever.

Glory to you, O Lord, glory to you!
~Amen.

### *The Jesus Prayer*

God greatly exalted him
and bestowed on him the name
that is above every name,
that at the name of Jesus
every knee should bend,
of those in heaven and on earth and under the
    earth,
and every tongue confess that Jesus Christ is Lord,
    to the glory of God the Father.

Philippians 2:9–11, NAB

#### PRAYER

Heavenly Father,
you appointed your only-begotten Son
to be the Savior of the human race
and named him Jesus.
Please look with favor on us
and may our respect for his holy name
lead to our seeing him in heaven.
We ask this through his precious name.
~AMEN.[20]

#### *THE MOST HOLY NAME OF JESUS*

The name of Jesus is both light and food.
Whenever we call it to mind we find fresh
strength. Whenever we meditate on it we find
ourselves enriched in virtue. It restores our
jaded senses, strengthens our virtuous habits,
and inspires chaste affections. All food is dry

and tasteless unless it is steeped in the oil of his name, insipid unless it is seasoned with this salt. Whatever I read has no taste for me unless I find the holy name of Jesus in it; no conversation has any interest for me unless I hear the name of Jesus in it. The name of Jesus is honey to the palate, music to the ear, a shout of gladness in the heart.

St. Bernard of Clairvaux (1090-1153)[21]

In fairly recent times, Eastern and Western Christians have gradually learned that they have spiritual treasures to share with one another. Among these is the Jesus Prayer, perhaps the finest gift of all. What was once the almost exclusive preserve of the Eastern Orthodox of Greece and Russia is in the process of becoming an experiential method of prayer for many Western Christians. Thanks to the modern translations of great spiritual classics like *The Way of the Pilgrim* and the even more profound *Philokalia*, and to the vast influence of the radiant homeland of prayer of Mount Athos, monks and other spiritual teachers, Catholic and Protestant, are now learning the deep way of prayer called the Jesus Prayer.

This is a spiritual discipline for devout believers who want to take seriously the Philippian quotation given above by putting into practice an almost immemorial manner of praying. It consists in saying the name of Jesus as a *mantra* to exclude all images and thoughts in order to allow unalloyed access to the Holy Spirit who dwells in our hearts. Other forms of prayer and meditation are good for those beginning to pray, but the Jesus Prayer is the key to inner prayer in all its depth. It requires an intense commitment to repeat the holy Name frequently and for some time, either alone or in a kind of formula like that used by so many of the Orthodox: "Lord Jesus Christ, Son of God, have mercy on me, a sinner." One must sit still and quietly repeat the holy Name over and over, patiently and persistently, while setting aside all images and words that try to interrupt it. This is easier said than done!

Here are some examples:

1. Set aside at least a half hour each day and say the Prayer carefully and quietly without interruption.
2. Say the Prayer for a few minutes before Mass.
3. At Holy Communion, say the Payer on the way to communion and even more insistently after receiving communion.
4. Before any form of private prayer, say the Prayer intensely for a few moments.
5. In times of confusion, disappointment, pain, or loneliness, set your heart on Jesus by saying the Prayer for some time.
6. As death approaches, say the Prayer relentlessly and with total trust in our Savior.

If a spiritual teacher is available, turn to him or her to process your experience, questions, and difficulties with the Prayer. And remember that the Jesus Prayer is not a gimmick or a trick but a profound gift of God that becomes more precious when used regularly and sincerely.[22]

## *A Prayer before Holy Communion*

Receiving the eucharistic body and blood of our Lord is the closest we shall come to Jesus in this life. Prayers before and after communion stir up our hearts to appreciate this divine gift.

My heart is wounded, O Master;
my zeal for you has melted away;
my love for you has changed me;
my utter devotion has bound me to you.
Let me be filled with your flesh;
let me be satiated with your living
   and deifying blood;
let me enjoy whatever is good;
let me delight in your divinity;
let me become worthy to meet you
as you come in glory,
and let me be caught up in the clouds
with all your chosen ones,
that I may praise, worship, and glorify you
in thanksgiving and doxology,
together with the Father
who is without beginning,
and your all-holy, good, and life-creating Spirit,
now and ever and unto the ages of ages.
Amen.

**St. John of Damascus (ca. 675–ca. 749)**[23]

## To Jesus in Our Tabernacles

The Eucharist is not only a festal meal but an abiding and personal presence of Jesus—body and blood, soul and divinity—in the tabernacle. No distant God is he! Whatever our needs, he is there for our worship and our consolation. "Amen. Come, Lord Jesus!" (Revelation 22:20).

The whole world should tremble and heavens
     rejoice,
when Christ, the Son of the living God,
is present on the altar in the hands of the priest.
What wonderful majesty! What stupendous
     condescension!
O sublime humility! O humble sublimity!
That the Lord of the whole universe, God and the
     Son of God,
should humble himself like this
and hide under the form of a little bread for our
     salvation.
Look at God's condescension, my brothers,
and pour out your hearts before him (Psalm 61:9).
Humble yourselves that you may be exalted by
     him (cf. 1 Peter 5:6).
Keep nothing for yourselves
so that he who has given himself wholly to you
may receive you wholly.

St. Francis of Assisi (1181–1226)[24]

## For True Devotion to the Blessed Sacrament

**ANTIPHON**

How sacred is the feast
in which you are our food,
the memorial of your sufferings
is celebrated anew,
our hearts are filled with grace,

and we are given a pledge
of the glory that is to come, alleluia!

You give us manna from heaven, alleluia!
~SENDING DOWN BREAD FOR US TO EAT,
ALLELUIA!

Let us pray for true devotion to the Blessed
Sacrament:

Lord Jesus,
high priest of the new and eternal covenant,
you feed our souls and bodies
with your sacramental body and blood,
and abide on our altars as our source
of ever-ready comfort and consolation.
Remind us each day that you are truly with us,
have us rejoice in your loving presence,
and steer us toward the doors of heaven.
Your reign is a reign for all ages.
~AMEN.

### To Our Most Holy Redeemer

Soul of Christ, make me holy.
Body of Christ, make me whole.
Blood of Christ, fill me with new life.
Water from the side of Christ, wash me clean.
Passion of Christ, make me strong.
O good Jesus, listen to me.
Within your wounds, hide me.
Keep me close to you.
From the evil enemy, defend me.

At the hour of death, call me to you,
That, with your saints,
I may praise you, now and for ever.
~Amen.[25]

## *Prayer to the Son of God*

You are the Son of God,
Lord Jesus,
and yet, for our sake, endured the cross
and became acquainted with grief.
And now you invite me
into lasting friendship with you.
For the sake of your holiness,
I would hold myself back,
but for the sake of your blood.
~Amen.

## *Prayer before the Blessed Sacrament*

O Jesus, present in the sacrament of the altar,
teach all nations to serve you with a willing heart,
knowing that to serve God is to reign.
May your sacrament, O Jesus,
be light to the mind,
strength to the will,
joy to the heart.
May it be the support of the weak,
the comfort of the suffering,
the wayfaring bread of salvation for the dying,
and, for all, the pledge of future glory.
Amen.

Pope John XXIII (1881–1963)[26]

### *A Visit to the Blessed Sacrament*

Lord Jesus, truly present in this tabernacle,
I believe in your holy presence here,
and that you are really Emmanuel, God-is-
    with-us.
You are with us today and every day,
the only begotten Son of the Most High,
full of grace and truth.
In union with all faithful Christians on earth
and with all the saints and angels in heaven,
I praise and thank and adore you with all my
    heart.
Trusting in your sacramental body and blood,
I appeal to you to enrich me with the grace
of your sacramental presence here and now,
that I may learn how to live, work, and pray
for all that is necessary to serve you well.
In honor of the Blessed Sacrament
that commemorates and makes present
your passion, death, and resurrection,
I devote my life and labors to you,
renew the holy promises of my baptism,
and commit myself to serving and loving others
for your precious sake.
In your mercy, Lord, hear my special prayers
in my time of need. . . .
Please console and comfort me in my sorrows
as I rely on your promise to hear all those
who pray to the Father in your name.

Hear and help me now, O Savior of the world,
as you live and reign with the Father,
in the unity of the Holy Spirit,
one God, for ever and ever.
~Amen.

## *Prayer in Full Faith*

Give me, good Lord, a full faith and a fervent
    charity,
a love of you, good Lord,
incomparable above the love of myself;
and that I love nothing to your displeasure
but everything in an order to you.

Take from me, good Lord, this lukewarm fashion,
or rather this cold manner of meditation
and this dullness in praying to you.
And give me warmth, delight, and life
in thinking about you.
And give me your grace to long for your holy
    sacraments
and specially to rejoice in the presence of your
    blessed body,
sweet Savior, in the holy sacrament of the altar,
and duly to thank you for your gracious coming.

St. Thomas More (1478–1535)[27]

## *A Prayer for Deliverance*

Deliver me, O Jesus,
From the desire of being loved,
From the desire of being extolled,

From the desire of being honored,
From the desire of being praised,
From the desire of being preferred,
From the desire of being consulted,
From the desire of being approved,
From the desire of being popular,
From the fear of being humiliated,
From the fear of being despised,
From the fear of suffering rebukes,
From the fear of being calumniated,
From the fear of being forgotten,
From the fear of being wronged,
From the fear of being ridiculed,
From the fear of being suspected.

*Mother Teresa*[28]

### *A Prayer for Help*

Have mercy, O Lord, on me in my futility.
Please grant me your wisdom
and fill me with your strength;
for I am a sinner,
weak in body,
wounded in spirit,
deficient in understanding.
~AMEN.

*Anonymous*

### *Hymn to the Sacred Heart of Jesus*

O Sacred Heart, for all once broken,
Your precious blood for sinners shed,

Those words of love by you were spoken
That raised to life the living dead.

O Heart, your love for all outpouring,
In pain upon the cross you bled;
Come now with life, our life restoring,
O Heart, by which our hearts are fed.

James Quinn, SJ[29]

### *Cast All Care on God Who Cares for You*
Come, heavy souls, oppressed that are
With doubts, and fears, and carking care.
Lay all your burdens down, and see
Where's One that carried once a tree
Upon his back, and, which is more,
A heavier weight, your sins, He bore.
Think then how easily He can
Your sorrows bear that's God and Man;
Think too how willing He's to take
Your care on Him, Who for your sake
Sweat bloody drops, prayed, fasted, cried,
Was bound, scourged, mocked, and crucified,
He that so much for you did do,
Will do yet more, and care for you.

Thomas Washbourne (1606–1687)

### *Doxology*
May the heart of Jesus in the most Blessed
      Sacrament
be praised, adored, and loved, with grateful
      affection,

at every moment, in all the tabernacles of the
    world,
even to the end of time. Amen.

## *Steal Away*

Steal away, steal away.
Steal away to Jesus.
Steal away, steal away home;
I ain't got long to stay here.

My Lord calls me;
he calls me by the thunder.
The trumpet sounds within my soul;
I ain't got long to stay here.

Green trees are bendin',
poor sinner starts a tremblin'.
The trumpet sounds within my soul;
I ain't got long to stay here.

Tombstones are burstin',
poor sinners start a tremblin'.
The trumpet sounds within my soul;
I ain't got long to stay here.

My Lord he calls me,
he calls me by the lightnin'.
The trumpet sounds within my soul;
I ain't got long to stay here.

Anonymous

## *Poem: Light Shines Out of Darkness*

God moves in a mysterious way
His wonders to perform;
He plants His footsteps in the sea,
And rides upon the storm.

Deep in unfathomable mines
Of never failing skill
He treasures up His bright designs,
And works His sovereign will.

You fearful saints, fresh courage take:
The clouds you so much dread
Are big with mercy, and shall break
In blessings on your head.

Judge not the Lord by feeble sense,
But trust Him for His grace;
Behind a frowning providence
He hides a smiling face.

His purposes will ripen fast,
Unfolding ev'ry hour;
The bud may have a bitter taste,
But sweet will be the flow'r.

Blind unbelief is sure to err,
And scan His work in vain;
God is His own interpreter,
And He will make it plain.

William Cowper (1731–1800)

### Jesus My Friend

Lord Jesus, friend of the human race,
and my personal friend, too:
You are close to me at every moment of my day,
You are teaching me how to live,
You show me how to be a friend to others,
You are helping me prepare for eternity.
You passed through the dark valley of death
but rose on Easter morning,
the light and life of the world.
Draw me to your sacred heart
and make me your personal disciple,
a friend of your Mother and of all the saints in
     glory.
Glory to God, alleluia! Glory to God!

### Hymn

All you who seek a comfort sure
In trouble and distress,
Whatever sorrow vex the mind,
Or guilt the soul oppress,
Jesus who gave himself for you
Upon the cross to die,
Opens to you his sacred heart;
Oh, to that heart draw nigh.

You hear how kindly he invites;
You hear his words so blest:
"All you that labor come to me,

And I will give you rest."
Christ Jesus, joy of saints on high,
The hope of sinners here,
Attracted by those loving words
To you we lift our prayer.

Edward Caswall (1814–1878)

# Devotions to Christ Crucified

We are all fascinated by the birth of Jesus in Bethlehem and his ministry throughout Galilee and Judea. He is the exorcist, the healer, and the preacher—but above all he is the Savior who died on the cross for us and rose again on the third day to bring all to the completion that God intended. We who believe and trust in the cross of Christ can handle any difficulty we experience in life. Jesus is the Rock on which we build our very existence.

## Antiphon

We adore your cross, O Lord,
and we praise and glorify your holy Resurrection,
for by the wood of the cross
you brought joy into the whole world.[30]

## The Sufferings of Jesus

St. Thomas Aquinas details the various sufferings that Jesus endured during his sacred passion.

Christ suffered from friends abandoning him;
in his reputation from the blasphemies hurled at
      him;
in his honor and glory, from the mockeries and
      the insults heaped upon him;
in things, for he was despoiled of his garments;
in his soul, from sadness, weariness, and fear;
in his body, from wounds and scourgings.

In his head he suffered from the crown of piercing
      thorns;

in his hands and feet, from the fixing of the nails;
on his face from the blows and spittle;
from the lashes over his entire body.
He also suffered in all his bodily senses;
in touch, by being beaten and nailed to the cross;
in taste, by being given vinegar and gall to drink;
in smell, by being fastened to the gibbet in a place
    called Calvary, reeking with the stench of
        corpses;
in hearing, by being tormented with the cries of
        blasphemers and scorners;
in sight, by seeing the tears of his mother and of
        the disciple whom he loved.

St. Thomas Aquinas (1225–1274)[31]

## *The Holy Face of Jesus*

The famous English mystic Julian of Norwich (1343–ca. 1423) visualizes the sufferings of Jesus in a way that permits us to see and feel the pains he endured.

I desire to suffer with him, living in my mortal body, as God would give me grace. And at this, suddenly I saw the red blood trickling down from under the crown, all hot, flowing freely and copiously, a living stream, just as it seemed to me as it was at the time when the crown of thorns was thrust down upon his blessed head. Just so did he, both God and man, suffer for me.

After this Christ showed me part of his Passion, close to his death. I saw his sweet face as it were

dry and bloodless, with the pallor of dying, then
more dead, pale and languishing, then the pallor
turned blue and then more blue, as death took
more hold upon his flesh. For all the pains that
Christ suffered in his body appeared to me in his
blessed face. . . . The long torment seemed to me
as if he had been dead for a week and had still
gone on suffering pain, and it seemed to me that
as if the greatest and the last pain of his Passion
was when his flesh dried up. . . . The blessed body
was left to dry for a long time, with the wrenching
of the nails and the sagging of the head and the
weight of the body, with the blowing of the wind
around him, which dried up his body and pained
him with cold, more than my heart can think
of. . . . This revelation of Christ's pains filled me
full of pains, for I know well that he suffered only
once, but it was now his will to show it to me and
fill me with its recollection. . . .

In this I saw part of the compassion of our Lady,
St. Mary, for Christ and she were so united in love
that the greatness of her love was the cause of the
greatness of her pain. For her pain surpassed that
of all others, as much as she loved him more than
all others.[32]

### *Jesus Crucified*
Jesus, when faith with constant eyes
Regards your wondrous sacrifice,

Love rises to an ardent flame,
And we all other hope disclaim.

With cold affections who can see
The lash, the thorns, the nails, the tree,
The flowing tears and purple sweat,
The bleeding hands, and head, and feet.

Look, saints, into his gaping side,
The cleft how large, how deep, how wide?
There issues forth a double flood
Of cleansing water, pard'ning blood.

From there, O soul, a balsam flows
To heal your wounds, and cure your woes;
Immortal joys come streaming down,
Joys, like his griefs, immense, unknown.

Thus I could ever, ever sing
The sufferings of my heavenly King:
With growing pleasure spread abroad
The mysteries of a dying God.

John Rippon[33]


### Christ Crucified

Sweet Christ,
the more we behold you
the more perfectly and purely do we love you,
and for love become one with you.
And as we become one with you by love
so we share in your sufferings, O Man of Sorrows,
and through grief become more united with you.

By this we come to the knowledge of God and of
ourselves
and are sincerely transformed into the love of the
Son of God.

St. Angela of Foligno (1248–1309)[34]

### Five Holy Cross Prayers

**ANTIPHON** The Lord of glory was crucified by the
rulers of this age for the salvation of the world.

1 Corinthians 2:8

Christ is victor, Christ is ruler,
~CHRIST IS LORD OF ALL.

Let us pray:

God of mercy and compassion,
whose loving kindness is without measure,
erase our sins by the blood of the cross
and free us from the power of the evil one
who prowls about seeking to devour us.
We ask this through Christ, our blessed Savior.
~AMEN.

**ANTIPHON** Jesus stretched out his hands on the
cross in order to embrace the ends of the earth.

By the power of your holy cross
~O SAVIOR, SAVE US.

Let us pray:

Lord Jesus Christ,
born for us in Bethlehem

dead for us on Calvary,
by the joyful crib and the sorrowful cross,
lift our hearts to your glorious resurrection,
O Lord of glory,
living and reigning with the Father,
in the unity of the Holy Spirit,
now and for ever.
~AMEN.

**ANTIPHON** The Word of God took flesh and hung
on the wood of the cross to recapitulate the
universe in himself.

From deep in the world of the dead I cried for help
~AND YOU HEARD ME.

Let us pray:
God of love,
you sent your only Son, not to condemn,
but to redeem the world,
By the four arms of the holy cross,
extend its saving power to the whole world
to save all those who put their trust in you;
through Christ Jesus our Lord.
~AMEN.

**ANTIPHON** O Cross of our Savior, you bind all
creation together, reaching to the heights of
heaven and sinking into the depths of the earth.

Into your hands, I commend my spirit, Lord,
~IT IS YOU WHO WILL REDEEM ME.

Let us pray:

Lord Jesus Christ,
by the power of your holy cross,
uproot all evil tendencies in our hearts
and plant in us all righteous impulses,
that we may praise, thank, and bless you,
in union with all the saints,
now and for ever.
~Amen.

**ANTIPHON** Cross of victory, planted in the heart of
the earth but bearing fruit in heaven, you are the
beginning and the end of God's mysteries.

Proclaim to the nations:
~The Lord reigns from the tree of the
    cross!

Let us pray:

Righteous God,
when Jesus cried out to you on the cross
you saved him from the depths of the grave
and made him the Savior of the world.
By his pierced and bleeding wounds,
wash away our sins in the blood and water
that poured from his sacred heart
and bring us to new life in his Holy Spirit.
We ask this through the same Christ our Lord,

who lives and reigns with you and the Spirit,
now and for ever.

~AMEN.

### *Prayer to Jesus Crucified*

Lord Jesus Christ, Son of the living God,
set your passion, your cross, and your death
between your judgment and our souls,
now and at the hour of our death.
In your great goodness,
grant mercy and grace to the living
and forgiveness and rest to the dead,
to the Church and to the nations,
peace and concord,
and to us sinners,
life and glory without end.

~AMEN.[35]

### *To the Five Wounds of Jesus*

The executioners nailed Jesus to the cross with three
great spikes through his hands and feet. After his death
a Roman officer pierced his heart with a spear. During
his long agony a faithful few stood beside him while
others jeered at him and scorned him. In all of life's
hardships, let us stand by the cross with his mother
Mary, Mary Magdalene, and the beloved disciple, con-
templating the five wounds and the precious blood of
Jesus, as we try to set our faith and hope in God our
Rescuer.

As St. Peter tells us, "You know that you were
ransomed from the futile ways inherited from your
ancestors, not with perishable things like silver or gold,
but with the precious blood of Christ, like that of a lamb

without defect or blemish. He was destined before the foundation of the world, but was revealed at the end of the ages for your sake. Through him you have come to trust in God, who raised him from the dead and gave him glory, so that your faith and hope are set on God" (1 Peter 1:18–21).

## I. To the Wound in the Right Hand

Blest be † the holy Wound in the right hand
  of Jesus, our crucified Savior!
~AMEN.

| READING | WHITE AS WOOL | ISAIAH 1:18–20 |

Come now, let us argue it out, says the LORD: though your sins are like scarlet, they shall be like snow; though they are red like crimson, they shall become like wool. If you are willing and obedient, you shall eat the good of the land; but if you refuse and rebel, you shall be devoured by the sword; for the mouth of the LORD has spoken.

### RESPONSORY PSALM 51

Create in me a clean heart, O God,
~AND PUT A NEW AND RIGHT SPIRIT WITHIN ME.

Purge me with hyssop, and I shall be clean;
wash me, and I shall be whiter than snow.
Hide your face from my sins,
and blot out all my iniquities.
~CREATE IN ME A CLEAN HEART, O GOD,
  AND PUT A NEW AND RIGHT SPIRIT WITHIN ME.

Create in me a clean heart, O God,
and put a new and right spirit within me.
Cast me not away from your presence,
and take not your Holy Spirit from me.
~CREATE IN ME A CLEAN HEART, O GOD,
   AND PUT A NEW AND RIGHT SPIRIT WITHIN ME.

**PRAYER**
Good and gracious God,
by the wound of love in the right hand
of your dear Son, our Savior,
you show us how merciful you are
in forgiving and forgetting our sins.
Though our sins are like scarlet,
make them whiter than snow;
though they are as red as crimson,
make them as clean as wool,
for you wash us in the blood of Jesus
and make us acceptable in your sight.
Blest be Jesus, true God and true Man.
~AMEN.

## II. To the Wound in the Left Hand
Blest be † the holy Wound in the left hand
   of Jesus, our crucified Savior!

~AMEN.

READING    FREED BY HIS BLOOD    REVELATION 1:5–7

To him who loves us and freed us from our sins by
his blood, and made us to be a kingdom, priests

serving his God and Father, to him be glory and dominion for ever and ever. Amen. Look! He is coming with the clouds; every eye will see him, even those who pierced him; and on his account all the tribes of the earth will wail. So it is to be. Amen.

## RESPONSORY PSALM 130
With the Lord
~THERE IS GREAT REDEMPTION!

Out of the depths I cry to you, O Lord!
Lord, hear my voice!
Let your ears be attentive
to the voice of my supplications!
~WITH THE LORD THERE IS GREAT REDEMPTION!

If you, O Lord, should mark iniquities,
Lord, who could stand?
But there is forgiveness with you,
that you may be worshipped.
~WITH THE LORD THERE IS GREAT REDEMPTION!

## PRAYER
Good and gracious God,
by the wound of love in the left hand
of your dear Son, our Savior,
have mercy on us all
and take away every sin from our hearts.
Save us from the time of trial
and deliver us from the evil one
who roams around like a roaring lion

seeking to devour us.
By the power of his precious wounds,
save us from all that may threaten
our commitment to Jesus the Messiah
and bring us under the shadow of his cross.
Blest be Jesus, true God and true Man!
~AMEN.

### III. To the Wound in the Right Foot

Blest be † the holy Wound in the right foot
   of Jesus, our crucified Savior!
~AMEN.

| READING | RESULTS OF THE PASSION | 1 PETER 2:9–10 |
|---------|------------------------|----------------|

You are a chosen race, a royal priesthood, a holy
nation, God's own people, in order that you may
proclaim the mighty acts of him who called you
out of darkness into his marvelous light. Once you
were not a people, but now you are God's people;
once you had not received mercy, but now you
have received mercy.

### RESPONSORY PSALM 36

With you
~IS THE FOUNTAIN OF LIFE, O LORD,
IN YOUR LIGHT WE SEE LIGHT.

Your steadfast love, O Lord, extends to the
      heavens,
your faithfulness to the clouds.

Your righteousness is like the mighty mountains,
your judgments are like the great deep;
O Lord, you save humans and animals!
~WITH YOU IS THE FOUNTAIN OF LIFE, O LORD,
IN YOUR LIGHT WE SEE LIGHT.

O God, how precious is your steadfast love!
All people take refuge in the shadow of your wings.
They feast on the abundance of your house,
and you give them to drink from the river of your
        delights,
~WITH YOU IS THE FOUNTAIN OF LIFE, O LORD,
IN YOUR LIGHT WE SEE LIGHT.

#### PRAYER

Good and gracious God,
by the wound of love in the right foot
of your dear Son, our Savior,
have mercy on us and absolve all our sins.
Through this wound of love,
grant us the gift of true repentance
with profound sorrow for all our sins.
You are the fountain of life, O Lord,
and in your light we see light
to walk in Christ's footsteps
that lead by the straight and narrow path
to the heavenly home prepared for us.
Blest be Jesus, true God and true Man.
~AMEN.

### IV. To the Wound in the Left Foot

Blest be † the holy Wound in the left foot
   of Jesus, our crucified Savior!

~AMEN.

|  | BLOOD | HEBREWS |
|---|---|---|
| READING | AND WATER | 10:19–22 |

My friends, since we have confidence to enter
the sanctuary by the blood of Jesus, by the new
and living way that he opened for us through the
curtain (that is, through his flesh), and since we
have a great priest over the house of God, let us
approach with a true heart in full assurance of
faith, with our hearts sprinkled clean from an evil
conscience and our bodies washed with pure water.

### RESPONSORY PSALM 141 AND 142

Let my prayer arise before you like incense,

~THE LIFTING UP OF MY HANDS LIKE AN EVENING
   OBLATION.

With my voice I cry to the Lord,
I make supplication;
Before the Lord I tell my trouble,
I pour out my complaint.
When my spirit is faint,
you know my way.

~LET MY PRAYER ARISE BEFORE YOU LIKE
   INCENSE, THE LIFTING UP OF MY HANDS LIKE
   AN EVENING OBLATION.

Bring me out of prison,
so that I may give thanks to your name!
The righteous will surround me,
for you will deal richly with me.
~Let my prayer arise before you like
    incense, The lifting up of my hands like
    an evening oblation.

**Prayer**
Good and gracious God,
by the wound of love in the left foot
of your dear Son, our Savior,
have mercy on us and absolve all our sins.
Through this wound of love,
deliver me from every trial and tribulation,
from every fear and temptation,
so that we may serve you wholeheartedly
and hold fast to you in our dying hour
by the intercession of your sorrowful Mother
and of all the saints in glory.
Blest be Jesus, true God and true Man.
~Amen.

## V. To the Wound in the Side
Blest be † the holy Wound in the side
    of Jesus, our crucified Savior!
~Amen.

So they asked Pilate to have the legs of the crucified men broken and the bodies removed. Then the soldiers came and broke the legs of the first and of the other who had been crucified with him. But when they came to Jesus and saw that he was already dead, they did not break his legs. Instead, one of the soldiers pierced his side with a spear, and at once blood and water came out. (He who saw this has testified so that you also may believe. His testimony is true, and he knows that he tells the truth.)

### RESPONSORY PSALM 22

They have pierced my hands and my feet;
~I CAN COUNT ALL MY BONES.

My God , my God, why have you forsaken me?
Why are you so far from helping me,
from the words of my groaning?
O my God, I cry by day, but you do not answer;
and by night, but find no rest.
~THEY HAVE PIERCED MY HANDS AND MY FEET;
I CAN COUNT ALL MY BONES.

I am poured out like water,
and all my bones are out of joint;
my heart is like wax,
within my breast;
my tongue sticks to my jaws;

you lay me in the dust of death.
~THEY HAVE PIERCED MY HANDS AND MY FEET;
I CAN COUNT ALL MY BONES.

To the One seated on the throne and to the Lamb
be blessing and honor and glory and might
for ever and ever!
~THEY HAVE PIERCED MY HANDS AND MY FEET;
I CAN COUNT ALL MY BONES.

**PRAYER**
Good and gracious God,
by the wound of love in the side
of your dear Son, our Savior,
have mercy on us and absolve all our sins.
Through this wound of love,
you show your great kindness
both to the Roman centurion
and to all sinful souls.
By the precious blood and water
that poured from your pierced heart,
deliver us from every evil,
past, present, and still to come,
and conduct us in safety
to our heavenly home.
Blest be Jesus, true God and true Man.
~AMEN.

## Hail, Sacred Heart of Jesus
Hail, Heart of my Jesus: save me!
Hail, Heart of my Creator: perfect me!

Hail, Heart of my Savior: deliver me!
Hail, Heart of my Judge: pardon me!
Hail, Heart of my Father: govern me!
Hail, Heart of my Master: teach me!
Hail, Heart of my King: crown me!
Hail, Heart of my Benefactor: enrich me!
Hail, Heart of my Pastor: guard me!
Hail, Heart of my Brother: stay with me!
Hail, Heart of my Incomparable Goodness:
    have mercy on me.
Hail, most Loving Heart: inflame me!
Amen.

St. Margaret Mary Alacoque (1647–1690)

## *To the Sacred Heart of Jesus*

O my God!
I offer you all my actions of this day
for the intentions and the glory of the Sacred
    Heart of Jesus.
I desire to sanctify every beat of my heart,
by uniting them to its infinite merits,
and I wish to make reparation for my sins
by casting them into the furnace of its merciful
    love.
O my God!
I ask you for myself and for those I hold dear
the grace to fulfill your holy will perfectly,
to accept for love of you
the joys and sorrows of this passing life,

so that we may one day be united in heaven
for all eternity. Amen.

St. Thérèse of Lisieux (1873–1897)

## *Litany of the Sacred Passion*

This litany may be used in conjunction with the devotion to the five wounds or as a separate devotion. We kneel before the cross to worship all that Jesus has done for us in his atrocious sufferings and ask that we may share them in some manner.

Lord Jesus, at the Last Supper you knew
    that Judas, one of the Twelve, would betray you:

~GOOD LORD, DELIVER US FROM FALSE FRIENDS
    AND TREACHERY.

Lord Jesus, during the supper, you humbly
    washed the feet of your disciples:

~GOOD LORD, MAKE US MEEK AND HUMBLE OF
    HEART.

Lord Jesus, at the Last Supper you gave us
    the sacrament of your broken body
    and outpoured blood:

~GOOD LORD, WE WORSHIP THE SEAL
    OF THE NEW AND ETERNAL COVENANT.

Lord Jesus, you asked your disciples to watch
    and pray with you in the Garden of
      Gethsemane:

~GOOD LORD, KEEP US AWAKE AND WATCHFUL
    WITH YOU.

Lord Jesus, at your arrest all your friends fled in
   fear
   and deserted you:
~GOOD LORD, GIVE US COURAGE IN TIME OF
   TRIAL.

Lord Jesus, you were falsely accused
   and condemned for speaking the truth
   before Annas and Caiaphas, the high priests:
~GOOD LORD, MAY WE SPEAK TRUTH
   IN THE FACE OF INJUSTICE.

Lord Jesus, in the courtyard of the high priest,
   Simon Peter swore three times
   that he did not know you:
~GOOD LORD, MAKE US FAITHFUL IN TIME
   OF TEMPTATION.

Lord Jesus, Pilate traded you for a murderer
   and handed you over to crucifixion:
~GOOD LORD, HAVE MERCY ON US SINNERS.

Lord Jesus, you were beaten, mocked,
   and humiliated by Pilate's soldiers:
~GOOD LORD, MAY WE SUFFER GLADLY FOR YOUR
   SAKE.

Lord Jesus, on the cross you were taunted
   and derided as King of the Jews:
~GOOD LORD, MAY WE ALWAYS LIVE IN
   OBEDIENCE TO YOU.

Lord Jesus, on the cross you forgave your enemies:

~GOOD LORD, GIVE US THE GRACE TO FORGIVE OURS.

Lord Jesus, from the cross you promised paradise
to a repentant criminal:

~GOOD LORD, MAKE US LONG FOR PARADISE AND ETERNAL BLISS.

Lord Jesus, from the cross you confided
your Blessed Mother to your beloved disciple:

~GOOD LORD, MAKE US CHILDREN OF MARY.

Lord Jesus, you cried out in agony
to your Father and died with a loud cry:

~GOOD LORD, HAVE MERCY ON US, NOW AND AT THE HOUR OF OUR DEATH.

Lord Jesus, the Roman centurion
recognized you as the Son of God:

~GOOD LORD, MAY WE ALWAYS PRAISE AND EXALT YOU AS OUR BLESSED SAVIOR.

Lord Jesus, you were taken down from the cross
and laid in the arms of your sorrowful Mother:

~GOOD LORD, ENTRUST US TO THE CARE OF YOUR BLESSED MOTHER.

Lord Jesus, Joseph of Arimathea
wrapped your body in a linen shroud
and laid you in his rock-hewn tomb:

~GOOD LORD, GRANT US THE GIFT OF TEARS AT THE MEMORY OF YOUR SUFFERING, DEATH, AND BURIAL.

Lord Jesus, the women who had followed you
    from Galilee watched as you were put to rest
    in the tomb:
~GOOD LORD, WE AWAIT WITH JOY YOUR
    GLORIOUS RESURRECTION ON THE THIRD
    DAY.

Pause for our special intentions.

We adore you, O Christ, and we bless you,
~FOR BY YOUR HOLY CROSS YOU HAVE REDEEMED
    THE WORLD.

Let us pray:

Lord Jesus Christ,
you were fastened with nails
to the wood of the cross
and raised on high for all to see.
As the sun grew dark and the earth quaked,
you surrendered your spirit to your Father,
descended among the dead,
broke open the gates of hell,
and freed those bound in darkness.
As angel choirs rejoiced,
you were raised to life again on the third day,
destroying death by your own death
and canceling the power of sin.
By these mighty deeds on our behalf,
rescue us from our blindness and tepidity,
inspire us anew by your Holy Spirit,
and lead us into a life of prayer and service

worthy of your awesome sacrifice,
O Savior of the world,
living and reigning with the Father,
in the unity of the Holy Spirit,
one God, for ever and ever.
~AMEN.

May the glorious passion of our Lord Jesus Christ
† bring us to the joys of paradise.
~AMEN.

### The Mother of Sorrows

O teach those wounds to bleed
In me, me, so to read
This book of loves, thus writ
In lines of death, my life may copy it
    with loyal cares.
O let me here, here, claim shares!
Yield something in thy sad prerogative,
    Great Queen of griefs, and give
    Me too my tears; who, though all stone
Think much that thou should'st mourn alone.

Richard Crashaw (1613–1649)

### Easter Day

The dazzling intensity of Jesus' return from the dead is
God's promise of our triumph over sin and death and all
of life's difficulties. Christ is risen! He is risen, indeed!

Most glorious Lord of lyfe, that on this day,
Didst make thy triumph over death and sin:

And having harrowed hell, didst bring away
Captivity thence captive us to win:
This joyous day, deare Lord, with joy begin,
And grant that we for whom thou didst dye
Being with thy deare blood clene washt from sin,
May live for ever in felicity.
And that thy love we weighing worthily,
May likewise love thee for the same againe:
And for thy sake that all life deare didst buy,
With love may one another entertayne.
So let us love, deare Love, lyke as we ought,
Love is the lesson which the Lord us taught.

Edmund Spenser (1552–1599)

**PRAYER**

Glorious Lord of life,
you rose again on the third day
to restore the world to felicity.
By the dynamism of your stunning resurrection,
adopt us into your triune family
that we may be your loving children,
now and for ever.

~AMEN.

# Prayers to the Blessed Virgin Mary

Jesus' Father is our Father and his Mother is our Mother. The coming of the eternal Word of God in the womb of Mary signals the perfect conjunction of the human and the divine and unites us by grace to the Holy and Undivided Trinity. Devotion to the mother of God is at the heart of the Catholic faith and recognizes her as "our life, our sweetness, and our hope" *(Salve Regina)*. Let us turn to her for protection. She listens to our prayers and helps us in all our needs *(Sub tuum praesidium)*.

This quotation from the famous mystic Julian of Norwich will inspire us to true devotion to our Lady:

*God brought our Lady to my understanding. I saw her spiritually in her bodily likeness, a simple, humble maiden, young in years, of the stature which she had when she conceived. Also God showed me part of the wisdom and truth of her soul, and in this I understood the reverent contemplation with which she beheld her God, marveling with great reverence that he was willing to be born of her who was a simple creature created by him. And this wisdom and truth, this knowledge of her creator's greatness and of her own created littleness, made her say meekly to the angel Gabriel: "Behold me here, God's handmaiden." In this sight I saw truly that she is greater, more worthy, and more fulfilled than everything else which God has created, and which is inferior to her. Above her is no created thing, except the blessed humanity of Christ.*[36]

### *The Canticle of Mary*

Like our Lord's Sermon on the Mount, Mary's Magnificat upsets all worldly values: a lowly woman, Mary, is blessed by all generations; the rich and the proud are put down; the poor and the humble are exalted.

My soul proclaims the greatness of the Lord,
my spirit rejoices in God my Savior,
for you, Lord, have looked with favor on your
     lowly servant.

From this day all generations will call me blessed:
    you, the Almighty, have done great things for
     me
    and holy is your name.
    You have mercy on those who fear you,
    from generation to generation.

You have shown strength with your arm
and scattered the proud in their conceit,
casting down the mighty from their thrones
and lifting up the lowly.
You have filled the hungry with good things
and sent the rich away empty.

You have come to the aid of your servant Israel,
to remember the promise of mercy,
the promise made to our forebears,
to Abraham and his children for ever.

Luke 1:46–55

## PRAYER

Let us put our complete trust in Mary:

Holy mother of God,
you are our model of faith
and of complete submission to the Father.
By your faith, trust, and obedience,
and by your fervent prayers of intercession,
give us all the virtues displayed in your life of
      faith
and draw us close to your immaculate heart
that worships our God with such perfection.
Blest be the great mother of God, Mary most holy!
~AMEN.

St. Bernardine of Siena (1380–1444)[37]

## *Sub Tuum Praesidium*

This is the earliest surviving prayer *to* Mary, probably of Egyptian origin, late second century. Pope Paul VI referred to it as "the well-known prayer *Sub tuum praesidium*, venerable for its antiquity and admirable for its content."[38]

We turn to you for protection,
holy Mother of God.
Listen to our prayers
and help us in our needs.
Save us from every danger,
glorious and blessed Virgin.[39]

## Ave, Maris Stella

This is the classic hymn sung at evening prayer on most feasts of the Virgin Mary; "Mary help us live by faith."

Praise to Mary, heaven's gate,
Guiding star of Christians' way,
Mother of our Lord and King,
Light and hope to souls astray.

When you heard the call of God,
Choosing to fulfill his plan,
By your perfect act of love
Hope was born in Adam's clan.

Help us to amend our ways,
Halt the devil's strong attack,
Walk with us the narrow path,
Beg for us the grace we lack.

Mary, show your motherhood,
Bring your children's prayers to Christ,
Christ, your Son who ransomed us,
Who for us was sacrificed.

Virgin chosen, singly blest,
Ever faithful to God's call,
Guide us in this earthly life,
Guard us lest, deceived, we fall.

Mary, help us live by faith
So that we may see your Son,
Join our humble prayers to yours,
Till life's ceaseless war is done.

Praise the Father, praise the Son,
Praise the Holy Paraclete;
Offer all through Mary's hands,
Let her make our prayers complete.[40]

### Salve, Regina
This is the most famous of the Marian anthems sung at the end of night prayer, addressing Mary: "O clement, O loving, O sweet Virgin Mary."

Hail, holy Queen, Mother of mercy,
hail, our life, our sweetness, and our hope.
To you we cry, the children of Eve;
to you we send up our sighs,
mourning and weeping in this land of exile.
Turn then, most gracious advocate,
your eyes of mercy toward us;
lead us home at last
and show us the blessed fruit of your womb, Jesus:
O clement, O loving, O sweet Virgin Mary.[41]

### Te Matrem Laudamus
We praise you as our Mother,
    we acclaim you as our blessed Lady.
All the earth reveres you,
    the Eternal Father's daughter.

The hosts of heaven and all the angelic powers
    sing your praise:
the angels join in the dance,
the archangels applaud, the virtues give praise,

the principalities rejoice, the powers exult,
the dominations delight, the thrones make
        festival,
the cherubim and seraphim cry out unceasingly:

*Holy, holy, holy is the great mother of God,*
    *Mary most holy;*
*Jesus, the blessed fruit of your womb,*
    *is the glory of heaven and earth.*

The glorious choir of apostles,
    the noble company of prophets,
    the white-robed army of martyrs,
    all sing your praise.

The holy church throughout the world celebrates
        you:
    the daughter of infinite Majesty,
    the mother of God's true and only Son,
    the bride of the Spirit of truth and consolation.

You bore Christ, the King of glory,
    the eternal Son of the Father.
When he took our nature to set us free,
    he did not spurn your virgin womb.

When he overcame death's sting,
    he assumed you into heaven.
You now sit with your Son
    at God's right hand in glory.

Intercede for us, O Virgin Mary,
    when he comes to be our judge.

Help your chosen people,
bought with his precious blood.
And bring us with all the saints
into glory everlasting.

Save your people, holy Virgin,
    and bless your inheritance.
Rule them and uphold them,
    now and for ever.

Day by day we salute you;
    we acclaim you unceasingly.
In your goodness pray for us sinners;
    have mercy on us poor sinners.

May your mercy sustain us always,
for we put our trust in you.
In you, dear Mother, do we trust;
defend us now and for ever.[42]

### *Salutation to the Blessed Virgin*

St. Francis, "a truly Catholic and apostolic man," built his personal life of prayer by a deep and warm devotion to the mother of God.

Hail holy Lady,
    Most holy Queen,
    Mary, Mother of God,
    Ever Virgin;
Chosen by the most Holy Father in heaven,
    Consecrated by him,
    With his most holy beloved Son
    And the Holy Spirit, the Comforter.

On you descended and in you still remains
    All the fullness of grace
    And every good.
Hail, his Palace!
Hail, his Tabernacle!
Hail, his Home!
Hail, his Robe!
Hail, his Handmaid!
Hail, his Mother!
And hail all holy virtues,
    Who, by the grace
    And inspiration of the Holy Spirit
    Are poured into the hearts of the faithful
    So that, faithless no longer,
    They may be made faithful servants of God
    Through you.

           St. Francis of Assisi, OFM (1181–1226)[43]

### *Memorare*

Remember, most loving Virgin Mary,
never was it heard
that anyone who turned to you for help
was left unaided.
Inspired by this confidence,
though burdened by my sins,
I run to you for protection.
Mother of the Word of God,
do not despise my words of pleading
but be merciful and hear my prayer.
Amen.[44]

### To Mary

Mary, dear mother, who gave God birth,
Help and care for us living here on earth.
  Govern, give us knowledge, and advise.
Since you're our mother too, maiden and wife,
Bathe away our sin; grant us good life
  And, in every need, help us to be wise.

Anonymous[45]

### A Marian Anthem

A great sign appeared in heaven:
a woman clothed with the sun,
with the moon under her feet,
and on her head a crown of twelve stars.

Revelation 12:1

In the Old Testament, the virgin Miriam
led her people to safety through the Red Sea;
In the New Testament, the Virgin Mary
was the chosen instrument of our salvation.

Happy are you, O Blessed Virgin Mary,
and worthy of all praise,
for out of you arose the Sun of righteousness,
Christ our Lord.

Holy Mother of God and ever-Virgin Mary,
you are the Temple of God,
the shrine of the Holy Spirit,
the only woman who fully pleased
our Lord Jesus Christ.

Hail, Mary, full of grace.
~The Lord is with you.

Let us pray:

Jesus, victorious Savior,
by the willing cooperation and heroic faith of
     Mary,
the valiant woman of the Gospel,
you crushed the head of our ancient enemy
and set all things under your feet.
By her continuing role in our salvation,
make her the pride and joy of believers
and the crowning glory of your church.
Your reign is a reign for all ages.
~Amen.

## To Our Lady of Consolation
Mary is the Mother of Mercy: refuge of sinners, comfort
of the troubled, and cause of our joy.

### Antiphon
Through a woman came death,
through a woman came life;
through Eve, our loss,
through Mary, our gain;
Eve succumbed to her seducer,
Mary brought forth our blessed Savior.

Lady of consolation and of all mercy,
~Pray for us in time of need.

Let us pray:

God of all consolation,
you blessed Mary with many joys and many
        sorrows
and gave her the strength to enjoy all the gifts
that you bestowed on her.
By her loving intercession,
help us to thank you for every assistance
and to ask your help in time of trouble.
In Jesus' name, we ask it.
~Amen.

## Antiphon of St. Francis

St. Francis prayed this supremely Trinitarian prayer to
Mary before beginning each "hour" of the Liturgy of the
Hours.

Holy Virgin Mary,
among all the women of the world,
there is none like you:
you are the daughter and the handmaid
of the most high King and Father of heaven;
you are the mother of our most holy Lord Jesus
        Christ;
you are the spouse of the Holy Spirit.
Pray for us with Saint Michael the Archangel
and all the powers of the heavens and all the saints
to your most holy and beloved Son, our Lord and
        Master.[46]

### *To Mary for the Sick*

Mary, health of the sick,
be at the bedside of all the world's sick people:
  of those who are unconscious and dying;
  of those who have begun their agony;
  of those who have abandoned all hope of a cure;
  of those who weep and cry out in pain;
  of those who cannot receive care because they
      are poor;
  of those who need to be resting
    but who are forced to work;
  for those who seek in vain for a less painful
      position in their beds;
  for those who pass long nights sleepless;
  of those who are tormented by the cares
    of a family in distress;
  of those who must renounce their plans for the
      future;
  of those, above all,
  who do not believe in a better life;
  of those who rebel and curse God;
  of those who do not know that Christ suffered
      like them
    and for them.[47]

### *To Our Sorrowful Mother*

**ANTIPHON** This child is destined for the falling and the rising of many in Israel, and to be a sign that will be opposed so that the inner thoughts of many will be revealed—and a sword will pierce your own soul too. Luke 2:34

A Roman soldier opened Jesus' side with his spear,
~AND PIERCED THE HEART OF HIS MOTHER.

Let us pray to our Lady of Sorrows:

Mary, Mother of Sorrows,
you experienced the poverty,
the rejection, and the misunderstanding
that was Jesus' fate.
As he hung on the cross,
you stood at his side
and watched him writhe in pain
and knew the desolation that wrung his soul.
By his precious blood and your tears,
stand at our side as we feel
some of the pressures and pains
that weigh on our lives in this world.
Be with us in trials and tribulations,
and hear our special prayers: (we state our needs).
Holy Mother of God be our Mother too,
now and always and for ever and ever.
~AMEN.

### *To Our Lady of Guadalupe*

In the western hemisphere the preeminent devotion to St. Mary is centered on the shrine of Guadalupe in Mexico City. Millions journey there each year to present their burdens to the Mother of Mercy. In a very special way she is the protector of the poor and oppressed, the comforter of the afflicted, the refuge of sinners, and the help of Christians.

**ANTIPHON** A great sign appeared in heaven:

a woman clothed with the sun,

with the moon under her feet,

and on her head a crown of twelve stars.

*Revelation 12:1*

Mary, you are more worthy of honor than the
    cherubim,

~AND FAR MORE GLORIOUS THAN THE SERAPHIM.

Let us pray to Mary of Guadalupe:

Holy Mother of God and Queen of heaven,

at Tepeyac you promised to show

all the nations of the world

your love, compassion, help, and protection.

Because you are our merciful Mother,

hear our laments, and remedy all our miseries,
    misfortunes, and sorrows.

Stamp your precious image on our hearts,

unveil your precious will for us,

and hold us in the hollow of your mantle

where you cross your hands,
now and always and for ever and ever.
~Amen.[48]

### *Prayer to Our Lady of Combermere*

O Mary,
you desire so much to see Jesus loved.
Since you love me,
this is the favour which I ask of you:
to obtain for me a great personal love of Jesus
        Christ.
You obtain from your Son whatever you please;
pray then for me,
that I may never lose the grace of God,
that I may increase in holiness and perfection
        from day to day,
and that I may faithfully and nobly fulfill the
        great calling in life
which your Divine Son has given me.
By that grief which you suffered on Calvary
when you beheld Jesus die on the Cross,
obtain for me a happy death,
that by loving Jesus and you, my mother, on earth,
I may share your joy in loving and blessing
the Father, the Son, and Holy Spirit for ever in
        Heaven.
Amen.[49]

### *A Prayer to St. Joseph in Time of Need*

Blessed Joseph, spouse of the Virgin Mary
and foster father of the Lord Jesus,
we confidently invoke your prayers for us.
Through the love that bound you to Mary
and by the paternal love you expressed to Jesus,
we humbly ask you to assist us in all our needs.
Watchful guardian of the holy family,
defend the chosen children of Jesus Messiah;
ward off from us every religious error,
and equip us to struggle with the powers of
      darkness.
As you once rescued the child Jesus from deadly
      peril,
protect the church from the snares of the enemy
and from every adversity.
Please shield each one of us from harm
so that, supported by your prayers and example,
we may be able to live a good Christian life,
die a holy death, and obtain eternal happiness in
      heaven.
Amen.

# II
# Prayers of Petition and Consolation

## Prayers for the Ill, Infirm, and Dying

During his public ministry, Jesus dedicated himself to healing the sick and even raised the dead three times. His church has always prayed for the sick, the ailing, and the dying and provided the anointing of the sick for healing and forgiveness, especially at the hour of death.

The church also offers many rituals, prayers, and Requiem Masses for our dear departed. Through them we are united to our friends and relatives who have died, just as we are attached to the saints in glory. The union of prayer and the dying, the dead, and the faithful departed is an intimate part of the communion of saints and a true sign of Catholic life and spiritual culture.

### Prayers for the Sick

Lord, God of mercies,
deign to stretch out your hands:
in your kindness, heal all the sick,

in your kindness, make them worthy of health,
deliver them from their present sickness;
in the name of your only-begotten Son,
grant them recovery;
let this holy name be their remedy
for health and restoration.
Through him, glory to you and power,
in the Holy Spirit,
now and for ever and ever.
~Amen.[50]

## In Time of Sickness

Lord Jesus, you suffered and died for me;
you understand suffering and share it with us.
Teach me to accept my pains,
to bear them in union with you,
and to offer them up for the forgiveness of my sins
and for the welfare of the living and the dead.
Calm my fears, increase my trust in you;
make me patient and cooperative with those who
    serve me,
and if it be your will, restore me to health,
so that I may live and work to your honor and
    glory,
and for the good of all.
~Amen.

## For Acceptance in Suffering

Lord of life and of death,
you love life and hate death.

You allowed your precious Son to die on the cross
but raised him in triumph on the third day.
Strengthen and comfort me
by the example of his passion and death,
alleviate my pains, if it be your will,
console me in my loss of mobility,
and give me the grace to bear my suffering
without complaining or questioning your wisdom.
Cheer me in my aches and pains
and make me an example of Christian patience
and holy resignation.
May Christ crucified be with me, now and for
        ever.
~AMEN.

### *For Healing*

Blessed be the LORD,
who has heard the sound of my pleading.
The LORD is my strength and my shield,
in whom my heart trusted and found help.
So my heart rejoices;
with my song I praise my God.

*Psalm 28:6–7, NAB*

Let us pray for good health:
Lord Jesus,
healer of our souls and bodies,
during your life on earth
you went about doing good,
healing every manner of sickness and disease,

strengthening, curing, and consoling.
You want to see us healthy and happy;
you are the enemy of sickness and disease,
and in and through you they are overcome and
    conquered.
Lay your healing hands upon us now,
so that we may praise you for ever.
~Amen.

## In Old Age

> And all the days of Methuselah were nine hundred
> sixty and nine years: and he died.
>
> Genesis 5:27

About the advanced age of the geriatric patriarchs and
their deaths the Bible is precise, but about the pains
and aches they must have suffered, it is noticeably
tight-lipped. What can be the meaning of old age and
the infirmities it brings? How hard it is to see those we
love diminished.

Teach us, Lord, to praise what is—
even that diminishment that age brings,
which is so terrible we can only hope to put it
    on your lap.
Help us pray more and more resolutely
the enigma and the terror that age is—
for every wrinkle, for every ache,
for the essential tremors and the palsies,
for the forgetfulness and the hesitation,
for the vacancy and the encroaching dementia,
for the pain and each failing ability, help us praise.

And, in that praise of time's good wreckage
    of the body,
let us see more fully the spirit's beauty;
in the suffering, let us see Christ crucified.
In the losses the aging suffer, teach us to see
how grandly they have filled our lives
    with grace and love.

In their approaching death, let us glimpse
    the Empty Tomb and the life
—theirs and ours—redeemed, transfigured,
    and glorified by your love.
~Amen.

J. Robert Baker

## For the Redemptive Use of Suffering

O Christ, my Lord, who for my sins did hang
        upon a tree,
grant that your grace in me, poor wretch, may still
        engrafted be.
Grant that your naked hanging there may kill in
        me all pride,
and care of wealth since you did then in such poor
        state abide.
Grant that your crown of prickling thorns, which
        you for me did wear,
may make me willing for your sake all shame and
        pain to bear.
Grant that your pierced hand, which did of
        nothing all things frame,

may move me to lift up my hands and ever praise
      your name.
Grant that your wounded feet, whose steps were
    perfect evermore,
may learn my feet to tread those paths which you
      have gone before.
Grant that your blessed grave, wherein your body
      lay awhile,
may bury all such vain delights as may my mind
      defile.
Grant, Lord, that your ascending then may lift my
      mind to thee,
that there my heart and joy may rest, though here
      in flesh I be.

St. Philip Howard (1557–1595)[51]

### *Thanksgiving for Recovery*

I praise you, LORD, for you raised me up
and did not let my enemies rejoice over me.
O LORD, my God,
I cried out to you and you healed me.
LORD, you brought me up from Sheol;
you kept me from going down to the pit.

Sing praise to the LORD, you faithful;
give thanks to God's holy name.
For divine anger lasts but a moment;
divine favor lasts a lifetime.
At dusk weeping comes for the night;
but at dawn there is rejoicing.

You changed my mourning into dancing;
you took off my sackcloth
and clothed me with gladness.
With my whole being I sing
endless praise to you.
O LORD, my God,
for ever will I give you thanks.

Psalm 30:1–6, 12–13, NAB

Let us give thanks for recovery from sickness:

God of mercy and compassion,
I cried out for mercy and you heard me
and became my helper.
I give you thanks for my recovery from sickness.
Please give me new strength to love and serve you
and to rejoice in my returning health.
Blessed be God for ever!
~AMEN.

### At the Hour of Death

As death approaches we show our love for one another by being present at the deathbed, at the anointing of the sick and the receiving of viaticum, and during the last hours. Often the dying cannot pray for themselves any longer and need our help. In Christian charity we must devote ourselves to praying with them and for them, over and over again until the last breath. We may turn to the basic prayers of a Christian: the Apostles' Creed, the Lord's Prayer, the Gloria Patri, the Hail Mary, and above all—slowly, quietly, and carefully—the holy rosary, that sweet summary of the Gospel. Toward the very end, the most valuable prayer is simply the holy name of JESUS.

### A Prayer for the Dying

Hail to thee! true Body sprung
From the Virgin Mary's womb!
The same that on the cross was hung,
And bore for us the bitter doom.

Thou whose side was pierced and flowed
Both with water and with blood,
Suffer us to taste of thee
In our life's long agony.

O kind, O loving One!
O sweet Jesus, Mary's Son.[52]

### Prayer of St. Macrina on Her Deathbed

Lord, you have taken the fear of death away from us.
The end of our life you have made the beginning
    of true life.
For a little while you will let our bodies rest in
    sleep,
and then with the last trumpet you will wake
    them from their sleep.
To free us from sin and from the curse laid upon us,
you took both the sins and the curse upon
    yourself.
When you shattered the gates of hell,
and trampled the Devil, death's lord, beneath your
    feet,
you cleared the way for our resurrection.

Set now an angel of light beside me
and bid him take my hand and lead me to the
    resting place
where there is water for refreshment.

If out of the weakness of human nature I have
    fallen
and sinned in word or deed or thought, forgive it
    me;
for you have power to forgive sins on earth.
When I am divested of my body,
may I stand before you with my soul unspotted;
receive it, blameless and faultless,
with your own hands.

St. Macrina (ca. 330–379), the sister of St. Basll the Great
and St. Gregory of Nyssa[53]

### For the Dying

Compassionate God, Father of mercies,
and God of all consolation,
you want the salvation of everyone
who believes in you and sets their hope on you.
In your boundless mercy,
look kindly on this dying person, Name,
who truly entrusts his/her soul to you.
Be his/her Savior, wash away his/her sins
in virtue of the passion and death of Jesus,
and be a merciful judge when he/she comes before
    you,

thoroughly washed in the blood of your Son,
whose reign is a reign for all ages.
~AMEN.[54]

## *For Those We Love*

Lord God,
we can hope for others nothing better
than the happiness we desire for ourselves.
Therefore, I pray you, do not separate me after
     death
from those I have loved tenderly on earth.
Grant that where I am they may be with me,
and that I may enjoy their presence in heaven
after being deprived of it so often on earth.
Lord God, I ask you to receive your beloved
     children
immediately into your life-giving heart.
After this brief life on earth,
give them eternal happiness.
~AMEN.

St. Ambrose of Milan (ca. 339–397)

## *Passing Over*

Lord Jesus, Light of the world,
I am passing over from the darkness of this world
into the bright light of eternity.
Thank you for guiding me this far
and take me one step further into your arms.
As my body weakens and my sight fails,

immerse me in the prayers of the saints
and guide and guard me by the holy angels;
may the glorious archangels, Gabriel, Michael, and
    Raphael
lead me through the gates of death
into the paradise for ever green,
and may I see you face-to-face in the beatific
    vision, soon! and for ever!
~Amen.

## For Momma, in a Coma at the Hour of Death

"I glorified you on earth by finishing the work that you
    gave me to do. . . . Holy Father, protect them in your
    name that you have given me." John 17:4, 11

Momma,
you know that we love you.
You've always been the heart of our family.
Teaching us, correcting us, loving us when we
    were small,
gathering us together to love and remember now
    that we are grown.

You loved us through our troubles, our rebellion,
    our mistakes.
You loved us in our joys, our celebrations, our
    success.
You kept us together, made us a family.
We are, such as we are, your life's work, and we
    are so blessed.

The time is coming, and we will need to go on
without you.
We know how much you want us to love each
other,
to care for each other.
Your work will go on. We promise to remain a
family.
And when we gather, we will remember you,
and how God blessed us all through you.

James M. Backes

### *In Paradisum*
May the angels lead us into paradise.
May the martyrs receive us at our coming
and conduct us into the holy city, Jerusalem.
May the choirs of angels receive us
and with Lazarus, who once was poor,
may we have eternal rest.[55]

### *Subvenite*
Come to our assistance, all you saints of God.
Come forth to meet us, you angels of the Lord.
Receive our souls and offer them in the sight of
the Most High.
May Christ who calls us receive us
and may the holy angels lead us into Abraham's
bosom.
Receive our souls and offer them in the sight of
the Most High.[56]

### For the Dying

Jesus, Mary, and Joseph, I give you my heart and
    my soul.

Jesus, Mary, and Joseph, assist me in my last
    agony.

Jesus, Mary, and Joseph, may I breathe forth my
    soul
  in peace with you. Amen.

### Abide with Me

Abide with me, fast falls the eventide;
The darkness deepens; Lord with me abide:
When other helpers fail and comforts flee,
Help of the helpless, O abide with me.

Swift to its close ebbs out life's little day;
Earth's joys grow dim; its glories pass away;
Change and decay in all around I see;
O thou who changest not, abide with me.

I need thy presence every passing hour;
What but thy grace can foil the tempter's power?
Who, like thyself, my guide and stay can be?
Through cloud and sunshine, Lord, abide with me.

I fear no foe, with thee at hand to bless;
Ills have no weight, and tears no bitterness;
Where is death's sting? Where, grave, thy victory?
I triumph still, if thou abide with me.

Hold thou thy cross before my closing eyes;
Shine through the gloom and point me to the
    skies;
Heaven's morning breaks, and earth's vain
    shadows flee;
In life, in death, O Lord, abide with me.

Henry Francis Lyte (1793–1847)

### Good Friday

Am I a stone, and not a sheep,
  That I can stand, O Christ, beneath Thy cross,
  To number drop by drop Thy Blood's slow loss,
And yet not weep?

Not so those women loved
  Who with exceeding grief lamented Thee;
  Not so fallen Peter weeping bitterly;
Not so the thief was moved;

Not so the Sun and Moon
  Which hid their faces in a starless sky.
  A horror of great darkness at broad noon—
I, only I.

Yet give not o'er,
  But seek Thy sheep, true Shepherd of the flock;
  Greater than Moses, turn and look once more
And smite a rock.

Christina Rossetti (1830–1894)

### The Cross

The sign of the cross shall appear in heaven
when our Lord shall come to judge the world,
and the servants of the cross,
who conformed themselves here in this life
to Christ crucified on the cross,
shall go to Christ their judge
with great faith and trust in him.

Thomas à Kempis[57]

### Peace at the Last

May God support us all the day long,
till the shades lengthen
and the evening comes
and the busy world is hushed
and the fever of life is over
and our work is done—
then in his mercy
may he give us a safe lodging
and a holy rest
and peace at the last. Amen.

Attributed to Cardinal John Henry Newman (1801–1890)

# Prayers for the Dead

Prayer for the dead is one of the most sympathetic of all devotions, uniting us with all our brothers and sisters in the one Body of Christ. Those who have gone before us into heavenly bliss are just Christians of a higher dimension; those being purged by the special mercy of God in purgatory are on their way to bliss; we who remain on earth have the privilege and responsibility of offering the holy sacrifice of the Mass and other forms of prayer in honor of the saints in glory and those on their way there. By our call to holiness we are urged to imitate the saints as we walk the narrow road to heaven and to pray that all come to their final unity in Christ our Lord.

## A Living Hope

Blessed be the God and Father of our Lord Jesus Christ. By his great mercy he has given us a new birth into a living hope through the resurrection of Jesus Christ from the dead, and into an inheritance that is imperishable, undefiled, and unfading, kept in heaven for you, who are being protected by the power of God through faith for a salvation ready to be revealed in the last time.

1 Peter 1:3–5

## For the Faithful Departed

### ANTIPHON

"I am the resurrection and the life.
Those who believe in me will live,
even though they die;

and those who live and believe in me
will never die!"

John 11:25–26

Holy is God, holy and strong,
~HOLY AND LIVING FOR EVER.

Let us pray:

God of mercy and compassion,
by your power Christ conquered death
and returned to you in glory.
May all who have gone before us in faith
share his victory and enjoy the vision
     of your glory for ever.
We make our prayer through Jesus Christ our
          Lord.
~AMEN.

Father of all consolation,
source of forgiveness and salvation for all,
hear our prayers for our dear departed Name, ARMANDO
By the intercession of the Blessed Virgin Mary,
of St. Michael the Archangel,
and of all the saints in glory,
may our friends, relatives, and benefactors
who have gone from this world
come to share eternal happiness
with the whole company of heaven.
Please grant this through Christ our Lord.
~AMEN.

May the souls of the faithful departed,
through the mercy of God, † rest in peace.
~Amen.

## Dies Irae

That day of wrath, that dreadful day,
When heaven and earth shall pass away,
What power shall be the sinner's stay?
How shall we meet that dreadful day?

When, shriveling like a parchèd scroll,
The flaming heavens together roll;
When louder yet, and yet more dread,
Swells the loud trump that wakes the dead;

Oh! On that day, that wrathful day,
When we to judgment wake from clay,
Be then the trembling sinner's stay,
Though heaven and earth shall pass away.[58]

## ⸸ Prayer

Absolve, Father of all mercies,
the souls of the faithful departed
from every bond of sin and error.
By the blood of Christ shed on the cross,
enable them to escape the Last Judgment
and enjoy the happiness of endless life;
by the merits of the same Christ our Savior.
~Amen.

## ✗ *Psalm 130: De Profundis*

This psalm (*De profundis* in Latin) is one of the penitential psalms and is used to commemorate the faithful departed in the Roman liturgy and in popular piety.

Out of the depths I call to you, LORD;
Lord, hear my cry!
May your ears be attentive
to my cry for mercy.

If you, LORD, mark our sins,
Lord, who can stand?
But with you is forgiveness
and so you are revered.

I wait with longing for the LORD,
my soul waits for his word.
My soul looks for the Lord
more than sentinels for daybreak.

More than sentinels for daybreak,
let Israel look for the LORD.
For with the LORD is kindness,
with him is full redemption.
And God will redeem Israel
from all their sins.

Psalm 130, NAB

## ✗ PSALM PRAYER

Let us pray for our departed family and friends:

Lord Jesus Christ,
you are the firstfruits of those

who have fallen asleep in death;
you are the resurrection and the life
for those who put their trust in you.
In you, Lord of life,
"Death is swallowed up in victory.
Where, O death, is your victory?
Where, O death, is your sting?"
By your precious blood,
the price of our redemption,
conduct our beloved family and friends
in safety to our heavenly home,
the paradise of love, peace, and joy,
for ever and ever.
~AMEN.

## O Christ, You Wept

O Christ, you wept when grief was raw,
and felt for those who mourned a friend;
come close to where we would not be
and hold us, numbed by this life's end.
ARMANDO
The well-loved voice is silent now
and we have much we meant to say;
collect our lost and wandering words
and keep them to the endless day.

We try to hold what is not here
and fear for what we do not know.
Oh, take our hands in yours, good Lord,
and free us to let go our friend.

In all our loneliness and doubt,
beyond what we can realize,
address us from your empty tomb
and tell us that life never dies.

John L. Bell and Graham Maule[59]

## X *For Our Dear Departed*

The souls of the righteous are in the hand of God,
and no torment will ever touch them.
In the eyes of the foolish they seemed to have
    died,
and their departure was thought to be a disaster,
but they are at peace.

Wisdom 3:1–4

ARMANDO

Let us pray for/our dear departed.

Lord Jesus Christ, King of glory,
deliver the souls of the faithful departed
from all the pains of death and hell.
May Michael the Archangel lead them into the
    holy light
that you promised to Abraham and Sarah
and their descendants in the faith.
May they come to a place of refreshment,
    light, and peace
with Mary, the Mother of God,
and the whole company of heaven,
and be one with you and your beloved Father,

in the unity of the Holy and Life-giving Spirit,
now and for ever.
~AMEN.

Merciful Father,
hear our prayers and console us.
As we renew our faith in your Son,
whom you raised from the dead,
strengthen our hope
that all our departed brothers and sisters
will share in his resurrection,
who lives and reigns with you and the Holy Spirit,
one God, for ever and ever.
~AMEN.[60]

### *Prayer for a Stillborn Child*
God our Creator,
from whom all life comes, comfort this family,
grieving for the loss of their hoped-for child.
Help them find assurance
that with you nothing is wasted or incomplete,
and uphold them in your love,
through Jesus Christ our Savior.
~AMEN.[61]

### *Prayer for a Dead Child*
Loving Father,
the sleep of death has robbed us
of our sweet child.
Thank you for her/his short life with us
and for holy baptism

that confirms our hope in you
and promises a fond reunion
in the heart of our blessed Savior,
who is our resurrection and our life
through all eternity.
~AMEN.

## *For Those Who Survive*

Father in heaven,
your Son Jesus Christ wept at the grave of
     Lazarus;
show your compassion to those who mourn.
Supply their needs,
and help them to trust for ever in your fatherly
     care.
~AMEN.[62]

May the souls of the faithful departed,
through the mercy of God, † rest in peace.
~AMEN.

## *Litany of the Faithful Departed*    ARMANDO

Let us constantly remember before God the souls of
our friends, relatives, and benefactors who have left
this life in the faith of Christ our Lord.

| | |
|---|---|
| Lord, have mercy. | ~LORD, HAVE MERCY. |
| Christ, have mercy. | ~CHRIST, HAVE MERCY. |
| Lord, have mercy. | ~LORD, HAVE MERCY. |
| God our Father in heaven, | ~HAVE MERCY ON US. |
| God the Son, | |
|   Redeemer of the world, | ~HAVE MERCY ON US. |

| | |
|---|---|
| God, the Holy Spirit, | ~HAVE MERCY ON US. |
| Holy Trinity, One God, | ~HAVE MERCY ON US. |
| Holy Mary, help of Christians, | ~PRAY FOR THEM. |
| Holy Mary, health of the sick, | ~PRAY FOR THEM. |
| Holy Mary, hope of the dying, | ~PRAY FOR THEM. |
| Holy Mary, mother of the church, | ~PRAY FOR THEM. |
| St. Joseph, hope of the sick, | ~PRAY FOR THEM. |
| St. Joseph, patron of the dying, | ~PRAY FOR THEM. |
| St. Joseph, protector of the universal church, | ~PRAY FOR THEM. |
| St. Michael the Archangel, conductor of souls, | ~PRAY FOR THEM. |
| St. Abraham and Sarah, ancestors in the faith, | ~PRAY FOR THEM. |
| St. John the Baptist, forerunner of Christ, | ~PRAY FOR THEM. |
| St. Peter and St. Paul, apostles and martyrs, | ~PRAY FOR THEM. |
| All you holy saints of God, | ~PRAY FOR THEM. |
| Son of God and Savior of the world, | ~GOOD LORD, DELIVER THEM. |
| From all sin and suffering, | ~GOOD LORD, DELIVER THEM. |
| From the rigor of your justice, | ~GOOD LORD, DELIVER THEM. |
| From the grasp of the devil, | ~GOOD LORD, DELIVER THEM. |
| From long and enduring pain, | ~GOOD LORD, DELIVER THEM. |
| From the loss of your holy presence, | ~GOOD LORD, DELIVER THEM. |
| By the mystery of your holy incarnation, | ~GOOD LORD, DELIVER THEM. |
| By your sacred birth in Bethlehem, | ~GOOD LORD, DELIVER THEM. |

By your holy Name,
Jesus/Savior, ~GOOD LORD, DELIVER THEM.
By your manifestation to
the gentiles, ~GOOD LORD, DELIVER THEM.
By your baptism, fasting, and trials
in the wilderness, ~GOOD LORD, DELIVER THEM.
By your preaching of the
Good News, ~GOOD LORD, DELIVER THEM.
By your transfiguration
on Mount Tabor, ~GOOD LORD, DELIVER THEM.
By your miracles of healing, ~GOOD LORD, DELIVER THEM.
By your raising of the dead, ~GOOD LORD, DELIVER THEM.
By your precious gift of the
Holy Eucharist, ~GOOD LORD, DELIVER THEM.
By your agony in the
Garden of Gethsemane, ~GOOD LORD, DELIVER THEM.
By your holy cross and
bitter passion, ~GOOD LORD, DELIVER THEM.
By your precious death
and burial, ~GOOD LORD, DELIVER THEM.
By your glorious resurrection
and wonderful
ascension, ~GOOD LORD, DELIVER THEM.
By your gift of the Holy Spirit,
our advocate and guide, ~GOOD LORD, DELIVER THEM.
At the hour of death
and on the day of
judgment, ARMANDO ~GOOD LORD, DELIVER THEM.
Pause for the names of our friends,
family, and benefactors.

Eternal rest grant unto them, O Lord,
~AND LET PERPETUAL LIGHT SHINE ON THEM.

℣ Let us pray:

O God, our Creator and Redeemer,
have pity on our dear departed
and grant them refreshment, light, and peace
in the bliss of your holy presence.
We ask this through Christ our Lord.
~Amen.

# Prayers in Times of Distress

## *Prayer in Despair*

Christians are sometimes driven to despair by personal or domestic disasters and may even feel that God has abandoned them. Jesus, too, fell into "great agony and distress" on the night before he was betrayed by Judas. In the Garden of Gethsemane "his sweat became like great drops of blood falling down on the ground" as he anticipated betrayal, desertion, torture, and death (Luke 22:44).

## *Psalm 13*

How long, LORD? Will you utterly forget me?
How long will you hide your face from me?
How long must I carry sorrow in my soul,
grief in my heart day after day?
How long will my enemy triumph over me?

Look upon me, answer me, LORD, my God!
Give light to my eyes lest I sleep in death,
Lest my enemy say, "I have prevailed,"
lest my foes rejoice at my downfall.

I trust in your faithfulness.
Grant my heart joy in your help,
that I may sing of the LORD,
"How good our God has been to me!"

Psalm 13, NAB

### PSALM PRAYER

Lord Jesus,
man of sorrows and acquainted with grief,

in the garden you prayed to your dear Father
in grief and fear but also with acceptance
and resignation to your holy will.
As we feel alone and in grief,
please deliver us from the terror of despair.
Even Jesus shed tears of blood in his agony
but still held on to God's loving hand;
may I do the same!
~AMEN.

### Help Me to Remember

> God is love, and those who abide in love
> abide in God, and God abides in them.
> 1 John 4:16

Gracious God,
I long to rest in your love but some days I get so
     distracted
by all that surrounds me:
Friends or family members whose lives are not
     working,
who are struggling with debt or addictions or loss,
or who are living in loveless relationships filled
     with despair.
Often I have no words—there are no words.
I have only the gift of my presence, my love, my
     prayers.
But too often these days my presence is insincere,
my love shallow, my prayers thin and frail.

I forget that you are here with them and with me.
I forget that in you, all things are possible.
I forget to rest, to trust, to depend on you.
Forgive me, God.
Remind me even as I pray, that you are already at
work
in the lives of those around me.
Help me to remember that just as a seed is planted
in the dark, safe soil so that new life can grow,
seeds of a different sort are sown in us,
and may well give birth to hope, love, trust, and
new life,
if only we allow them to be nourished by the gift
of your Spirit.
Such growth is not mine to direct or force or
manage.
What am I to do, O God?
Perhaps I am simply to trust, even when I doubt
anything can grow in the poor, damaged soil of
their lives.
Perhaps I am to reflect on the fact that I need you
as much as these others for whom I pray.
Hear my prayers, dear One, for all of us.
In the name of Christ, who came to earth
and chose to be one with us,
and knows us better than we know ourselves.
Amen.

Martha Carroll

### In the Time of Distress

In the hour of my distress,
When temptations me oppress,
And when I my sins confess,
   Sweet Spirit comfort me!

When I lie within my bed,
Sick in heart and sick in head,
And with doubts discomforted,
   Sweet Spirit comfort me!

When the tapers now burn blue,
And the comforters are few,
And that number more than true,
   Sweet Spirit comfort me!

When the judgment is revealed,
And that opened which was sealed,
When to Thee I have appealed,
   Sweet Spirit comfort me!

Robert Herrick (1591–1674)

### In Desolation

During his excruciating hours on the cross, Jesus gradually fell into great desolation and dereliction and finally called out to his Father, "My God, my God why have you abandoned me?" When we feel entirely alone and even abandoned by all human resources, we can pray Psalm 22 with him.

My God, my God, why have you abandoned me?
Why so far from my call for help,
from my cries of anguish?

My God, I call by day, but you do not answer;
by night, but I have no relief.

Yet you are enthroned as the Holy One;
you are the glory of Israel.
In you our ancestors trusted;
they trusted and you rescued them.
To you they cried out and they escaped;
in you they trusted and were not disappointed.

Psalm 22:2–6, NAB

**PSALM PRAYER**
Lord Jesus,
on the cross of bitter pain,
you cried out to your Father
from the depths of your misery and dejection.
May I stand with you in your sufferings of mind
    and body,
and still appeal to your mercy and compassion,
knowing that every hair of my head is counted by
    you
and that not even a sparrow falls from the sky
without you knowing it.
Lord, have mercy. Christ, have mercy. Lord, have
    mercy.

## In Time of Temptation

Try as we might, at times temptation seems to overwhelm us and try us beyond our powers. Even in the depths, we can call upon our heavenly Father, "Save us from the time of trial!" and be confident that we are heard without fail.

Compassionate God,
show your loving face to us
and remind us of Jesus on the cross:
the blood shed for us, the body broken for us,
the sacred heart pierced for us.
As confused and raddled as we might be
by the deceits, stratagems, and chaos
of the world, the flesh, and the devil,
help us in your mercy and tell us once again
that your very nature is to love us, forgive us,
and restore us to our baptismal innocence.
Blest be the God of mercy!
~Amen.

## In Time of Anxiety

I don't know what's going to happen
And I'm afraid.

I might fall and break my hip and never walk
again.
I might become senile and be a burden to
everyone.
The money might run out.
I might have a stroke and wake up with one side
of my face sagging.
I see these things happening all around me.
There seems to be no end of them.
And no end to the horror show that goes on
behind my eyes if I let it.
Help me not to let it.

Help me not to look ahead but to this day,
    to this hour, this minute.
If the present is difficult, help me cope with it.
If it is painful, help me bear it.
If it is empty, help me fill it.
If it is good, help me enjoy it.
Most of all, help me live it.

Elsie Maclay[63]

### *For the Unemployed*

What can try us more than unemployment? Seeing our talents wasted and our abilities untested, we come to feel completely disoriented and even worthless.

Creator God,
I need work to fulfill my talents and my other needs.
You have made me a co-creator with you
and I feel really frustrated by my joblessness.
At times I feel that other people despise me
and that I even despise myself for being without a
    job.
Please help me to feel my true worth in your sight
as I risk everything in my quest for work.
Help my family and friends to assist me and
    encourage me
to keep up my spirits, to open my mind to new
    opportunities.
May Jesus of Nazareth, a workman and son of a
    workman,
† bless and assist me.
God help me!

## For the Frustrated

Turn and twist as we may, life's disappointments and baffling encounters can frustrate us to the point of dismay and exhaustion. Just think of Jesus and his frustrating disciples and apostles. Try as he might, their obtuseness, jealousy, and even stupidity frustrated his many attempts to ready them for the reign of God. Even on the day of his ascension into heaven, after all he had said and done for them, they didn't get it! (Acts 1:6).

Compassionate God and Father,
you know exactly what pains, stymies, and
      frustrates me.
Help me to recognize that you esteem and love me
and want to give me what I need for a good life.
Show me the road to true success in life.
Help me to ponder the teaching of the Sermon on
      the Mount,
to accept its wisdom and its challenges,
and not to compromise them out of all
      consideration.
Show me the temptations of the world, the flesh,
      and the devil
that contradict the Gospel completely and in
      detail.
Teach me not just to call you, "Lord, Lord,"
but to accept your lordship in my life day by day
that I may come to peace and rest in your holy
      will for me.
~Amen.

### For the Mentally Afflicted

Lord Jesus, during your life on earth,
again and again you rescued the emotionally
and mentally afflicted from their distress.
Be with me in my hour of need,
deliver me from my suffering and embarrassment,
and help me to cooperate with my medical
    assistants
to manage, control, and/or heal my condition.
Be with my troubled family and friends
that they may understand and sympathize with
    me,
pray for me, and stand by me.
Jesus, exorcist, healer, and miracle worker,
I know you are Emmanuel, God-is-with-us,
and want the best for me;
may I unite all my sufferings with you,
   my crucified Redeemer.
I surrender myself to you and to your holy will,
today and every day of my life.
~Amen.

### Prayer of Submission

Be still, my soul; the Lord is on thy side;
Bear patiently the cross of grief or pain;
Leave to thy God to order and provide;
In every change he faithful will remain.
Be still, my soul: thy best, thy heavenly friend
Through thorny ways leads to a joyful end.

Be still, my soul; thy God doth undertake
To guide the future as he has the past.
Thy hope, thy confidence let nothing shake;
All now mysterious shall be bright at last.
Be still, my soul: the waves and winds still know
His voice who ruled them while he dwelt below.

Jane Lorie Borthwick (1813–1897)

## *Laid Off*

So when Joseph reached his brothers, they pulled
off his coat, the coat with long sleeves, that he was
wearing, and catching hold of him they threw him into
a well, an empty well with no water in it. They then sat
down to eat.

Genesis 37:24

Lord, I've been thrown down a well: laid off, fired,
    redundant.
Up to now I've been, like Joseph, "the man of
    dreams."
Now I'm bruised, at the bottom of a hole, looking
    up.
Wondering what I did here.
And my own brothers, having a party!

I don't know what's going to happen.
I might be lifted up just to be sold into slavery.
Or betrayed again or sent to jail.
I don't know your plan, or my part in it.

All I know is that it's just you and me in this hole.

Just stay with me whatever comes,
slavery or success,
ruin or riches.

I sure hope it's riches,
but I know that things didn't get better for Joseph
     until he understood,
"I do not count. It is God who will give an
     answer." Genesis 41:16

James M. Backes

### *For the Parents of Teenagers*

O my people, hear my teaching:
listen to the words of my mouth!
I will open my mouth in a parable;
I will utter dark sayings from of old,
things that we have heard and known,
that our ancestors have told us.
We will not hide them from their children,
but tell to the coming generation
the glorious deeds of the LORD, the might
and wonders God has wrought.

Psalm 78:1–4

Let us pray for the troubled and troubling:

Lord, Lord, how down I feel as a parent
when my teenagers look miserable
and turn on me and others in their misery.
No matter what I try to do for them,
I feel rejected and even despised by them.

Help me to remember that being a teen
is at least a mild form of insanity!
They suffer even more than we do
and lash out against us in their rage.
"Father, forgive them for they know not what they
        do!"
Give me long-suffering patience with them and
        with myself.
Being a parent has its joys but also its trials.
Our road to holiness, our narrow path to heaven,
is strewn with teens to tempt and try us.
God give us wisdom, courage, and firmness
for the long haul.
~Amen.

### *For a Troubled Family*
I lift my eyes to you,
who are enthroned in the heavens!
As the eyes of the servants
look to the hand of their master,
as the eyes of a maidservant
to the hand of her mistress,
so our eyes look to the Lord,
until God has mercy on us.

Psalm 123:1–2

Let us pray for peace in our family:

Lord Jesus,
for most of your life you lived in a family
whose members cherished one another

and devoted themselves to the glory of God.
Joseph, your foster father, was a workman;
Mary, your dear Mother,
accepted the incomparable task
of being the mother of the Messiah.
You lived together in the little towns of Bethlehem
and Nazareth, lived in exile in Egypt,
returned to Galilee,
and waited in expectation for the further plan of
God.
Son of God and Mary,
direct our eyes to their thirty years together
and help us to model our lives
on their harmonious togetherness.
~AMEN.

## In Time of Divorce
The sundering of partners meant for a lifetime together
is one of the saddest facts of life. We lament divorce
and its effects on children, friends, and family.

I hate divorce, says the LORD, the God of Israel,
and covering one's garment with violence, says the
LORD of hosts. So heed to yourself and do not be
faithless.

Malachi 2:16

PRAYER
God of all consolation,
in an earlier and lovelier time,
we vowed to love and live together for a lifetime,

to cherish and support one another,
and be friends together.
We lament and repent of what has happened
to destroy such hope and promise.
Forgive us, Lord, forgive us,
for being unable to keep our wedding vows
and for breaking the living icon of Christ and his
    Church.
May our friends stand by us in our distress
and never forget that we all bear heavy burdens.
We ask this through Christ, our blessed Savior.
~AMEN.

### *In Widowhood*

Anyone in a good marriage suffers painfully from the loss of a spouse. Widows and widowers need new affirmation and support from their friends and family and a fresh vision of the remainder of their lives. Many of them can discover ways of serving the church that were not open to them earlier.

O LORD, my heart is not lifted up,
my eyes are not raised too high;
I do not occupy myself with things
too great and too marvelous for me.

But I have calmed and quieted my life,
like a weaned child with its mother;
I am like a weaned child.

O Israel, hope in the LORD
now and forever.

Psalm 131

A married woman is not free as long as her husband lives; but if her husband dies, she is free to be married to any man she wishes, but only if he is a Christian. She will be happier, however, if she stays as she is. That is my opinion, and I think that I too have God's Spirit.

Let us pray for courage for a new day:

Holy Mary, mother of God,
you were probably widowed at an early age
and became dependent on Jesus and other
      relatives
for food, shelter, and support.
Good Mother, help me in my new state of life
and give me the strength to serve you in a new
      way.
You lost both a husband and a son
but under the Spirit's guidance became the mother
      of the Church.
May I joyfully accept my new role in life, take on
      new tasks,
and become more and more who I am in your
      sight.
May your dear Son be the center of my life,
your Church, my true family,
my vocation, my completion, my fulfillment.
~AMEN.

May the divine assistance † remain always with us,
and may the souls of the faithful departed
through the mercy of God rest in peace.
~AMEN.

### *Against Addiction*

Addictions to drugs and alcohol drag us down to a subhuman level, destroying friendships and other human relationships. Only Jesus can save us from such slavery!

I call upon you, for you will answer me, O God;
listen to me, hear my words.
Wondrously show your steadfast love,
O Savior of those who seek refuge
from their adversaries at your right hand.
Guard me as the apple of your eye;
hide me in the shadow of your wings,
from the wicked who attack me,
my deadly enemies who surround me.

Psalm 17:6–9

Let us pray for deliverance from drugs:

Merciful Savior,
by the precious blood of the cross
that poured from your pierced heart,
you are mighty enough to save even me
from my slavery to drugs.
You will my health and safety
and my return to family and friends.
O Savior of the world,

save me and mine
and make me fully human again.
Your reign is a reign for all ages!
~Amen.

## *A Final Prayer*

Finally, we must surrender ourselves to the Holy Trinity and long for the higher reaches of mystical prayer where God resolves all our doubts and perplexities and conducts us into the explanation that exceeds all words.

Trinity! Higher than any being, any divinity, any
    goodness!
Guide of Christians in the wisdom of heaven!
Lead us beyond unknowing and light, up to the
    farthest, highest peak of mystic scripture,
Where the mysteries of God's word lie simple,
    absolute, and unchangeable in the brilliant
    darkness of hidden silence.
Amid the deepest shadow they pour
    overwhelming light on what is most
    manifest.
Amid the wholly unsensed and unseen they
    completely fill our sightless minds with
    treasures beyond all beauty.[64]

# Prayers of Petition

## *Christ in Us*

Christ has no body on earth but yours, no hands
> but yours.

Your eyes are the eyes through which Christ's
> compassion is to look out on the world.

Yours are the feet with which He is to go about
> doing good,

and yours are the hands with which He is to bless
> us now.

St. Therese of Lisieux (1873–1897)

## *For Blessed Unity*

How good it is, how pleasant,
where the people dwell as one!
Like precious ointment on the head,
running down upon the beard,
upon the beard of Aaron,
upon the collar of his robe.
Like dew of Hermon coming down
upon the mountains of Zion.
There the LORD has lavished blessings,
life for evermore!

Psalm 133, NAB

Let us pray for unity and peace:

Giver of peace and lover of concord,
you want us to live in peace and charity

and show that we are real Christians.
Soften our hard hearts toward our neighbors
and give us the grace to love and serve them
generously and gratefully.
We ask this through Christ our Lord,
the friend of the human race.
~AMEN.

## For a Good Marriage

The most profound longings of the human heart are for a loving relationship with another human being. In the midst of the chaos of a secular, hedonistic, and acquisitive society, we have to pray and work for the restoration of Christian marriage where love can flourish, where children can enjoy the loving devotion of attentive parents, where old and young can learn from one another, and where people love and cherish one another for a lifetime.

## For the Blessings of Home

Unless the LORD build the house,
they labor in vain who build.
Unless the LORD guard the city,
in vain does the guard keep watch.

It is vain for you to rise early
and put off your rest at night,
to eat bread earned by hard toil—
all this God gives to his beloved in sleep.

Children too are a gift from the LORD,
the fruit of the womb, a reward.

Like arrows in the hand of a warrior
are the children born in one's youth.
Blessed are they whose quivers are full.

Psalm 127, NAB

Let us pray for a happy home:

Giver of all blessings,
teach us to be dependent on you,
putting our family under your protection.
Thank you for the fruit of the womb;
may they grow and prosper
and be faithful children of the Church of God
and a credit to their parents.
We ask this through Christ our Lord.
~Amen.

### For Peace and Quiet

The LORD is my shepherd;
there is nothing I lack.
In green pastures you let me graze;
to safe waters you lead me;
you restore my strength.

You guide me along the right path
for the sake of your name.
Even when I walk through a dark valley,
I fear no harm for you are at my side;
your rod and staff give me courage.

You set a table before me
as my enemies watch;

You anoint my head with oil;
my cup overflows.

Only goodness and love will pursue me
all the days of my life;
I will dwell in the house of the LORD
for years to come.

Psalm 23, NAB

Let us pray for confidence:

Jesus, Good Shepherd,
attentive, kind, and gentle with your people,
have us realize and explicitly acknowledge
that you are present for us at every moment.
Nothing escapes your friendly interest
and especially not in our darkest instants.
Remind us that the sacraments of initiation
—baptism, confirmation, eucharist—
are lifelong events, manifestations
of your ever-ready goodness and love.
~Amen.

## For Spouses

How wonderful it is, how pleasant,
for God's people to live together in harmony!
It is like the precious anointing oil
running down from Aaron's head and beard,
down to the collar of his robes.
It is like the dew on Mount Hermon,
falling on the hills of Zion.

This is where the Lord has promised his
    blessing—
life that never ends.

Let us pray for family harmony:

Blessed Trinity of Persons,
we have come together to honor you
by being an image of your unity.
Center our family on you in all we do.
May our hearts belong to you and to one another
for the fostering of unity and peace,
under the shadow of the cross of Jesus
and by the help of Mary and of all the saints in
    glory.
Glory to you, O God, glory to you!
~Amen.

### For Our Parish

Jerusalem, the City of Peace, is the ideal model
for our parish. Just as every good Israelite—Jesus,
Mary, and Joseph, for example—went on pilgrimage
three times a year to the holy temple in Jerusalem,
so we go to our parish church at least every Sunday.
It is the shrine of holiness where we hear the Gospel
preached, celebrate the Holy Eucharist, participate
in other forms of sacramental worship, and enjoy the
presence and talents of our fellow Christians.

I rejoiced when they said to me,
"Let us go to the house of the LORD."
And now our feet are standing

within your gates, Jerusalem.
Jerusalem, built as a city,
walled round about.
Here the tribes have come,
the tribes of the LORD,
As it was decreed for Israel,
to give thanks to the name of the LORD.

Here are the thrones of justice,
the thrones of the house of David.
For the peace of Jerusalem pray:
"May those who love you prosper!
May peace be within your ramparts,
prosperity within your towers."

For family and friends I say,
"May peace be yours."
For the house of the LORD, our God, I pray,
"May blessings be yours."

Psalm 122, NAB

Let us pray for the well-being of our parish:

Great God of the temple of heaven,
we praise and thank you for the baptismal font
and the holy altar of our parish church
where we meet the living Jesus
in the sacraments of initiation
and in Holy Communion.
Fill us with faith and fervor each Sunday
and give us the strength to carry out
the gospel message in our lives.

Good Lord, bless our priests and deacons
and all our fellow parishioners:
Peace on them, blessings be theirs!
through Jesus Christ our Lord.
~AMEN.

### *For Trust and Humility*

Pride is the root from which all the branches of sin proceed. Humility is, therefore, the remedy and the cure.

LORD, my heart is not proud;
nor are my eyes haughty.
I do not busy myself with great matters,
with things too sublime for me.
Rather, I have stilled my soul,
hushed it like a weaned child.
Like a weaned child on its mother's lap,
so is my soul within me.
Israel, hope in the LORD,
now and forever.

Psalm 131, NAB

Let us pray for the gift of humility:

Lord Jesus,
you humbled yourself by taking our nature
and even more in your passion and death
when you learned complete trust in your Father.
Since pride is the source of all sins,
please help us to true humility before you
and our fellow sinners.

Teach us that we are not the center of the universe
and that we make and will make many mistakes
as long as we live.
Repentance and humility are required of us all
and especially when we presume to stand before
     you in death.
Good Jesus, be with us in our hour of need.
~AMEN.

### For Holiness

Holy, mighty, and deathless God,
your strongest desire for us
is to grow in holiness day by day.
In holy baptism you planted the seed in us,
and urge us to feed and water it
until we become perfect in your sight.
Help us to stand at the heart
of the Catholic tradition of prayer:
give us warm devotion to the seven sacraments,
lead us into the heart of the Holy Scriptures,
and be with us in our daily prayers,
for you love humankind and our salvation.
~AMEN.

### For Perfect Love

A lawyer asked Jesus what is the first and greatest of
all the commandments of the Law, and we all know the
answer: "The Lord our God is Lord alone! You shall love
the Lord your God with all your heart, with all your soul,
with all your mind, and with all your strength" (Mark
12:29–30 NAB).

My God, I want to love you perfectly,
with all my heart, which you made for yourself,
with all my mind, which you alone can satisfy,
with all my soul, which longs to soar to you,
with all my strength, my feeble strength,
which shrinks from so great a task
and yet can choose nothing else
but spend itself in loving you.
Claim my heart; free my mind;
uplift my soul; reinforce my strength;
that where I fail, you may succeed in me
and make me love you perfectly,
through Jesus Christ, my Lord.[65]

### For Patience
Each of us is personally known and cherished by God.
Let us not override his plan for us by our impatience.

The steadfast love of the Lord never ceases;
God's mercies never come to an end;
they are new every morning;
your faithfulness is great.

You are all that I have
and therefore I will wait for you.
You, Lord, are good to those who wait for you,
to all those who seek you.
It is good to wait in patience
for the salvation of the Lord.

Lamentations 3:22–26

Merciful and faithful Lord,
teach us to wait in patience
for you to reveal your plan for us.
You hold us in the palm of your hand;
may we never forget it.
In Jesus' name we pray.
~AMEN.

## For Fresh Courage

Now and again we all need cheering up by a fresh
vision of God's love and concern for us. It gives us
strength to go on.

The wilderness and the dry land shall be glad,
the desert shall rejoice and blossom;
like the crocus it shall blossom abundantly,
and rejoice with joy and singing.
The glory of Lebanon shall be given to it,
the majesty of Carmel and Sharon.
They shall see the glory of the LORD,
the majesty of our God.

Say to those who are of a fearful heart,
~"BE STRONG, DO NOT FEAR!"

Isaiah 35:1–2, 4

PRAYER

Majestic God and Father,
your glory is revealed in nature and in grace,
and inspires confidence in our hearts.
Enlighten our minds and strengthen our wills

to embrace your plan for us
that leads us into eternal glory.
Blessed be God, now and for ever.
~Amen.

## For Perfect Confidence

One of life's greatest trials is the feeling that God is very far away and even possibly unapproachable and uncaring. The divine and infinite Word of God, the second Person of the Blessed Trinity, became human in our very flesh and blood precisely to assure us that God is ever present and ever caring. Jesus comes to us in Holy Communion in an unbreakable union with our very human selves and assures us by the sight of the sacramental signs that he is truly and perfectly present to and for us.

### Hymn

Your Body, Jesus, once for us was broken,
Your Blood outpoured to heal a broken world.
You rose from death in glory of the Spirit,
Your royal flag victoriously unfurled.

So now these signs of Bread and Wine, retelling
Your dying gift, your living self proclaim.
Until you come in splendor at earth's ending
Your people, Lord, your hidden presence here
    acclaim.

James Quinn, SJ[66]

Let us thank Jesus for the gift of his eucharistic
    presence:

Gracious Savior,
we praise and thank you for the cup of blessing,
a sharing in your precious blood,
and the bread we break,
a sharing in your broken body.
We rely completely on these perfect gifts
that come to us from your love alone.
In any time of pain, loneliness, or sorrow,
we profess our faith in your sacramental presence
and entrust ourselves totally to your care.
Feed us with your body and blood,
transform us by your presence,
and make us rejoice in your blessed promise
that you will be with us to the end of the age.
Blessed be Jesus in the most holy Sacrament of the
    Altar!
~Amen.

## For the Fullness of Our Baptism

Our Savior fulfilled all righteousness by taking on the sin of the world as he was immersed in the Jordan by John the Baptist (Matthew 3:15). Later in his ministry he instituted the sacrament of baptism by which we die to the death of sin and rise to new life in Christ. Our faith assures us of God's undying hold on us and of our right to claim the ever-present power of God and our privilege to renew the promises of our baptism.

Jesus came from Nazareth of Galilee and was baptized by John in the Jordan. And just as he was coming up out of the water, he saw the heavens

torn apart and the Spirit descending like a dove
on him. And a voice came from heaven, "You are
my Son, the Beloved; with you I am well pleased."
And the Spirit immediately drove him out into the
wilderness.

Mark 1:9–12

**RESPONSE**
Jesus was in the wilderness forty days,
~TEMPTED BY SATAN; AND ANGELS WAITED ON
HIM.

Let us pray:

Holy Father of Jesus,
by virtue of the baptism of your dear Son,
inspire us to renew the vows of our own baptism
and so recommit ourselves to your service.
You will never forget our baptism
and our membership in the body of Christ.
May your beloved Son be our strength,
now and for ever.
~AMEN.

## For the Gift of Wisdom
Wisdom is a breath of the power of God,
and a pure emanation of the glory of the
        Almighty;
therefore nothing defiled gains entrance into her.
For she is a reflection of eternal light,

a spotless mirror of the working of God,
and an image of his goodness.

Although she is but one, she can do all things,
and while remaining in herself, she renews all
	things;
in every generation she passes into holy souls
and makes them friends of God, and prophets;
for God loves nothing so much as the person
	who lives with wisdom.

She is more beautiful than the sun,
and excels every constellation of the stars.
Compared with the light she is found to be
	superior,
for it is succeeded by the night,
but against wisdom evil does not prevail.
She reaches mightily from one end of the earth
	to the other,
and she orders all things well.

Wisdom 7:24—8:1

Let us pray for the gift of wisdom:
Lord Christ, you are Wisdom itself
and the Light of the world.
Give us a taste of the wisdom
that makes us friends of God
and even prophets of your gospel.
May holy wisdom order all things well.
Her reign is a reign for all ages.
~AMEN.

### For Divine Correction

Your immortal spirit is in all things.
Therefore you correct little by little
    those who trespass,
and you remind and warn them of the things
    through which they sin,
so that they may be freed from wickedness
and put their trust in you, O Lord.

*Wisdom 12:1–2*

Let us pray for the Lord's correction:

Lord of holiness and righteousness,
thank you for the sacred teaching
of your holy Catholic Church,
that recalls us to the pristine norms of holiness
that Jesus wants for us.
Revive the indwelling Spirit of holiness
that came to us in our baptism,
give us the grace of our first fervor,
and the love of your commandments.
Blest be Jesus, the teacher of holiness!
~AMEN.

### For Christian Friendship

Faithful friends are a sturdy shelter:
whoever finds one has found a treasure.
Faithful friends are beyond price;
no amount can balance their worth.
Faithful friends are lifesaving medicine;
and those who fear the Lord will find them.

Those who fear the Lord
  direct their friendship aright,
for as they are, so are their neighbors also.

Sirach 6:14–17

Let us pray for good friends:

Good Father,
your treasured gift of friendship
is a life-giving medicine for our ills.
Give us true friends who will stand by us
in Christian fellowship and support,
for standing alone is a danger to our souls.
Your Son had good friends on earth;
we need them too.
We ask this through Christ our Lord.
~AMEN.

### For Divine Wisdom

It is a happy person who is concerned with
    Wisdom
and who uses good sense.
Anyone who studies the ways of Wisdom
will also learn secrets.
Go after Wisdom like a hunter
looking for game.
Look into her windows
and listen at her doors.
Camp as close to her house as you can,
and you will have a fine place to live.
Build your home there,

safe behind her protecting branches,
and shaded from the heat.

Sirach 14:20; 15:3f, TEV

Let us pray for divine wisdom:

Holy God,
you sought us first
but we are obliged to seek you
and the wisdom you have for us
in the teachings of Jesus.
Help us read the Gospels
with attention and devotion,
asking for the wisdom and insight
that they provide to all earnest seekers.
We ask this through Christ our Lord.
~AMEN.

## For Reverence in Prayer

Shortsighted as we are, we often forget the incomparable majesty of God and the awe and reverence God deserves, both in liturgical worship and in private prayer. Reality demands that we join the exalted seraphim that surround the heavenly throne in awe-filled worship of the Supreme Being.

In the year that King Uzziah died, I saw the Lord sitting on a throne, high and lofty; and the hem of his robe filled the temple. Seraphs were in attendance above him; each had six wings: with two they covered their faces, and with two they

covered their feet, and with two they flew. And
one called to another and said:
"Holy, holy, holy is the LORD of hosts,
the whole earth is full of his glory."
The pivots on the thresholds shook at the voices of
those who called, and the house filled with smoke.

Isaiah 6:1–4

Let us pray for the gift of reverence:

We bow down in adoration before you,
O holy, mighty, and deathless God,
and humble ourselves before you,
recognizing that you are high and lofty
and that we are weak and pitiful.
Great God and Savior of the human race,
we prostrate ourselves before your majesty
and beg you for the gift of devout worship.
You are our first beginning and our last end
and our destiny lies in recognizing
that central fact of our lives.
Blest be the Holy and Undivided Trinity,
now and always, and for ever and ever.
~AMEN.

# For Repentance and Forgiveness

"Forgive us our sins as we forgive those who sin against us." That is the only condition for winning forgiveness. Nevertheless, forgiveness and repentance often do not come easily. We turn in prayer to our heavenly Father to open our hearts even to our enemies. Listen to Jesus in the Sermon on the Mount: "Stop judging, that you may not be judged. For as you judge, so will you be judged, and the measure with which you measure will be measured out to you" (Matthew 7:1–2 NAB).

## Noverim Me, Noverim Te

Lord Jesus, may I know myself and know you,
   and desire nothing except you.

May I hate myself and love you.
May I do everything for the sake of you.
May I humble myself and exalt you.
May I think of nothing except you.
May I die to myself and live in you.
May I receive whatever happens as from you.
May I banish self and follow you,
   and ever desire to follow you.
May I fly from myself and fly to you,
   that I may deserve to be defended by you.
May I fear for myself and fear you,
   and be among those who are chosen by you.
May I distrust myself and trust in you.
May I be willing to obey on account of you.
May I cling to nothing but to you.
May I be poor for the sake of you.

Look upon me that I may love you.
Call me that I may see you
and ever and ever enjoy you. Amen.

St. Augustine of Hippo Regius (354–430)

### For the Gift of Repentance

Turn back to the Lord and forsake your sins;
pray in his presence and lessen your offense.
Return to the Most High and turn away from
     iniquity,
and hate intensely what he abhors.

How great is the mercy of the Lord,
and his forgiveness to those who return to him!
For not everything is within human capability,
since human beings are not immortal.

Sirach 17:25–26, 29–30

Let us pray for God's mercy:

Compassionate God,
your very nature is to forgive us
and embrace us
even after we have gone far astray.
Thank you for your mercy
and for the future give us the capacity
to hate what you abhor
and love what you find dear.
We ask this through Christ our Lord.
~AMEN.

### *For Repentance and Forgiveness*

Come now, let us argue it out,
  says the LORD:
though your sins are like scarlet,
  they shall be like snow;
though they are red like crimson,
  they shall become like wool.
If you are willing and obedient,
  you shall eat the good of the land;
but if you refuse and rebel,
  you shall be devoured by the sword;
  for the mouth of the LORD has spoken.

Isaiah 1:18–20

Let us pray for the gift of tears:

Merciful Savior,
you forgive and forget our sins
at the moment we repent before you.
No matter how stupid or malicious they were,
they should vanish from our hearts too.
If we trust your word, "Your sins are forgiven!"
we must not doubt that they are in truth.
Kneeling at the foot of the cross,
we look to your five precious wounds
for complete healing of our sinful tendencies
and for the strength to remedy their effects.
Your reign, Lord Jesus, is a reign for all ages!
~AMEN.

## *Prayer to Be Forgiven*

"Go your way, and from now on do not sin again."
John 8:11

Lord Jesus Christ, whose will all things obey:
Pardon what I have done,
and grant that I, a sinner, may sin no more.
I believe that, though I do not deserve it,
you can cleanse me of all my sins.
Send your Spirit into my innermost being
to take possession of my soul and body.
Without you I cannot be saved,
but under your protection,
I find hope and confidence as I long for salvation.
Of your great goodness help and defend me.
Guide my heart, almighty God,
that I may remember your loving presence
by day and by night.
~AMEN.

## *The Trisagion of Sanctification*
After a heartfelt act of contrition and/or the sacrament
of reconciliation, putting us at peace with God, this
prayer sets our feet on the path of holiness again.

Holy, mighty, and living God, born of the Virgin
        Mary:
~HAVE MERCY ON US.
Holy, mighty, and living God, crucified for us:
~HAVE MERCY ON US.

Holy, mighty, and living God, who rose from the
    dead for us:
~HAVE MERCY ON US.

Glory to the Father, and to the Son, and to the
    Holy Spirit:
~AS IT WAS IN THE BEGINNING, IS NOW, AND WILL
    BE FOR EVER. AMEN.

I sign † myself with the cross of Christ
who died for me and for my salvation.
Renew in me the gift and cleanliness of my
    baptism,
the sweet chrism of my confirmation,
the blessed taste of your Body and Blood
    on my tongue in Holy Communion.
May your grace-filled sacraments,
won for us by the blood of our Savior,
be our life, our peace, and our joy,
now and for ever.
~AMEN.

### Christ in the Universe
Nothing comes into being except in Christ and nothing
is sustained except through him. May we see his face
everywhere!

I see his blood upon the rose
And in the stars the glory of his eyes.
His body gleams amid eternal snows,
His tears fall from the skies.

I see his face in every flower;
The thunder and the singing of the birds
Are but his voice—and carven by his power
Rocks are his written words.

All pathways by his feet are worn,
His strong heart stirs the everlasting sea,
His crown of thorns is twined with every thorn,
His cross is every tree.

Joseph Mary Plunkett (1887–1916)[67]

## *To Christ Crucified*

My God, I am not moved to love Thee
By the heaven that Thou hast promised me,
Nor does the fear of hell move me
To leave off offending Thee.
Thou movest me, Lord, I am moved to see Thee
Nailed to that cross, and mocked.
Thy wounded body moves me.
I am moved by the anguish of Thy death.
I am moved, in a word, by Thy love, in such a way
That though there were no heaven,
   I still should love Thee,
And though there were no hell, I still should fear
      Thee.
Thou needest give me no reason to love Thee,
      Lord,
For though I did not hope for all I hope for
I still should love Thee as I love Thee now.

Anonymous[68]

## The Seven Deadly Sins and Their Remedies

The classical sins and the roots of sin undermine and destroy our Christian life, set a bad example for our neighbor, and make us harmful to other people. We avoid and remedy them by embracing their opposites, and by trusting in the mercy and power of God to deliver us from them.

PRIDE sets us at the center of the universe
and exalts us even above the Lord our God.
It makes us hateful to our fellow human beings
and has Satan rejoice in our shame.

Merciful Lord,
grant us the grace of HUMILITY
by which we come to understand
our true position in God's scheme of things
and help us to be kind and gentle
to our family, friends, and neighbors.
Amen.

COVETOUSNESS draws us to grasp at things created
and to despise the things of heaven.
It makes us envy our neighbors
and lust after what they possess;
burn with desire for what passes away
and forget the treasures of heaven.

Merciful Lord,
grant us the grace of DETACHMENT

and prepare us for heaven by detaching us
even from the good things of earth.
Amen.

LUST makes us greedy for sexual pleasure
and wary of the commitments of love.
It causes us to despise the dignity of our neighbors
by lusting after their bodies as if they had no
     souls.

Merciful Lord,
grant us the gift of CHASTITY
and ready us for fraternal charity
in spirit and in truth.
Amen.

ANGER fills us with resentment and hatred
and the desire to harm our neighbor.
It exalts our passion and poisons our opinions
about those with whom we live and work
and causes us to judge harshly
and to always think others in the wrong.

Merciful Lord,
grant us the gift of MEEKNESS
that makes allowances for other people
and always remembers that they too
bear heavy burdens.
Amen.

**GLUTTONY** makes us overly concerned about eating
and drinking
and careless of our personal health.
It neglects sobriety and careful choices about food,
is overly concerned about its taste
and careless about its quality.
It causes ill health, painful diseases, and an early
death.

Merciful Lord,
grant us the gift of TEMPERANCE
that makes us sober, watchful, and discerning
that we may enjoy our meals
but not be enslaved by them.
Amen.

**ENVY** makes us begrudge the good of our neighbor
and hanker after the possessions of other people.
It makes us consumers rather than the children of
God
and makes us jealous and resentful of the gifts,
attainments, and virtues of those who surround
us.

Merciful Lord,
grant us the gift of THE LOVE OF NEIGHBOR
that has us rejoice in the good of others
and admire their virtues rather than their
belongings.
Amen.

SLOTH renders us indolent, inactive, and careless
of our own good and that of others.
It makes a virtue out of neglect and apathy in
religion
and a lack of involvement in the welfare of others.
It makes us poor citizens of our country,
lax members of our families,
and neglectful of our friends.

Merciful Lord,
awaken us to the joy of A DILIGENT AND ACTIVE
LIFE
that glorifies God and serves humankind
with zeal, ardor, and dedication.
Amen.

## *How Virtue Drives Out Vice*
Where there is Love and Wisdom,
there is neither Fear nor Ignorance.
Where there is Patience and Humility,
there is neither Anger nor Annoyance.
Where there is Poverty and Joy,
there is neither Cupidity nor Avarice.
Where there is Peace and Contemplation,
there is neither Care nor Restlessness.
Where there is Fear of God to guard the dwelling,
there no enemy can enter.
Where there is Mercy and Prudence,
there is neither Excess nor Harshness.

St. Francis of Assisi (1181–1226)[69]

### Invocation

Come, my Way, my Truth, my Life:
such a way as gives us breath;
Such a truth as ends all strife;
such a life as conquers death.

Come, my Light, my Feast, my Strength:
such a light as shows a feast;
Such a feast as mends in length;
such a strength as makes a guest.

Come, my Joy, my Love, my Heart:
such a joy as none can move;
Such a love as none can part;
such a heart as joys in love.

George Herbert (1593–1633)

### Who Is There to Understand?

All the fears I need to name but am too scared to
        say:
all the shame for what I've done, which nothing
        can allay;
all the people I've let down and lost along the way;
all the hate I still remand.

 Must these torment me to the end of time?
 Who is there to understand?

All the wasted years in which I struggled to be
        free;
all the broken promises that took their toll on me;
all the love I should have shown and all I failed
        to be;

all I longed to take my hand.
    Must these torment me to the end?
    Who is there to understand?

What the cause of pain is and, much more, the
        reason why;
what my final hour will bring, how suddenly I'll
        die;
what the future holds for those I'll miss, for whom
        I cry;
what, too late, I might demand.
    Shall these torment me to the end of time?
    Who is there to understand?

"All the wrong you now admit, I promise to
        forgive;
all that you regret you are not sentenced to relive;
all the love you've never known is mine alone to
        give;
you, my child, are understood.
    So do not fear all that is yet to be:
    heaven is close and God is good."

John L. Bell [70]

### To Know My Sins

Now gracious Lord,
as Thou givest me Thy grace to know my sins,
so give me Thy grace not only in word but in heart
        also,
with very sorrowful contrition to repent them
and utterly forsake them.

And forgive me those sins also in which,
by mine own default, through evil affections and
    evil custom,
my reason is with sensuality so blinded
that I cannot discern them for sin.
And illumine, good Lord, mine heart,
and give me Thy grace to know them
and to acknowledge them,
and forgive me my sins negligently forgotten,
and bring them to my mind
with the grace to be purely confessed of them.

St. Thomas More (1478–1535)[71]

### *For the Forgiveness of Sins*

You willed that your glorious head should be
    wounded
  by a crown of thorns:
  by it forgive what sin soever I have committed
    by hearing and seeing.

You willed that your sacred hands should be
    pierced by nails:
  by them forgive what sin soever I have
    committed
    by unlawful touch.

You willed your precious side should be pierced
    by a spear:
  by it forgive what sin soever I have committed
  by unlawful thoughts in the heat of lust.

You willed your blessed feet should be fastened
      by nails:
  by them forgive what sin soever I have
      committed
  by the going of feet swift to evil.

You willed that your whole body should be
      stretched forth
  on the cross:
  by it forgive what sin soever I have committed
  by the means of all my members.

Lancelot Andrewes (1556–1626)[72]

# III
# Prayers of Gratitude and Thanksgiving

## Hymns of Praise

We don't praise God for his sake but for ours. By setting our minds and hearts on the magnificent goodness of God we enter into the true sphere of reality, ground ourselves in the beauty of God, and learn how to rejoice and be glad even in the midst of our sins and sorrows.

### *Thank You Jesus!*

"The first duty of a Christian is to return thanks."
St. Ambrose of Milan (ca. 339–397)

Thank you, Jesus, for the gift of the Good News.

Thank you, Jesus, for the gift of the community of faith.

Thank you, Jesus, for the gift of the seven sacraments.

Thank you, Jesus, for the gift of life and hope.

Thank you, Jesus, for the gift of relatives and
   friends.

Thank you, Jesus, for the gift of health and
   strength.

Thank you, Jesus, for the gift of many talents.

Thank you, Jesus, for the gift of serving others.

Thank you, Jesus, for the gift of thanksgiving for
   everything!

To the Ruler of the ages, immortal, invisible, the
   only wise God,
be honor and glory, through Jesus Christ,
for ever and ever. Amen.

### *Prayer of Thanksgiving*

Gracious and loving God,
you command us to pray for what we need
but also to thank you for what we receive.
Make us ever thankful for the gift of human life
and for new life in Christ our Savior.
Make us grateful for his personal choice of us,
for the heavenly home he has destined for us,
for the companionship of his Blessed Mother
and of all the saints and angels,
for his personal presence in our tabernacles,
for Christian friends and relatives to encourage us,
and for his persistent call to holiness.
Blessed be the name of Jesus, now and for ever.
~Amen.

## A General Prayer of Thanksgiving

Almighty God, Father of all mercies,
we your unworthy servants give you humble
      thanks
for all your goodness and loving-kindness
to us and to all whom you have made.
We bless you for our creation, preservation,
and all the blessings of this life;
but above all for your immeasurable love
in the redemption of the world by our Lord Jesus
      Christ;
for the means of grace, and for the hope of glory.
And, we pray, give us such awareness of your
      mercies,
that with truly thankful hearts we may show forth
    your praise,
not only with our lips, but in our lives,
by giving up ourselves to your service,
and by walking before you
in holiness and righteousness all our days;
through Jesus Christ our Lord,
to whom, with you and the Holy Spirit,
be honor and glory throughout all ages.
~Amen.[73]

## Litany of Praise and Thanksgiving

O God, our heavenly Father,
the giver of every good and perfect gift,
we lift up to you our voice in thanksgiving;

we praise you for the life you have given us,
and for the service to which you have appointed
us,
for the knowledge of your will,
and the inspiration of your love:
~WE PRAISE YOU, O GOD.

For the work we have strength to do,
for the truth we are permitted to learn;
for whatever good there has been in our past lives,
and for the hope that leads us on to better things:
~WE THANK YOU, O GOD.

For revealing your presence in nature,
and the tokens of your wisdom and power,
in the least as in the greatest;
for every moment of closer communion with your
Spirit
in all that is fair and glorious in the universe:
~WE THANK YOU, O GOD.

For home and friends,
for all the comfort and gladness of our lives;
for encouragements to duty,
for help in time of temptation;
for sympathy in sorrow,
for the peace that is gained through strife,
and the rest that comes after toil:
~WE THANK YOU, O GOD.

Make us worthy of all your mercies,
and give us the grace to know and do your holy
will,

so may your kingdom come, and your will be
>    done,
on earth as it is in heaven.
~AMEN.[74]

### *Holy Father of Glory*

Now to the Father who created each creature,
Now to the Son who paid ransom for his people,
Now to the Holy Spirit, Comforter of might:
Shield and heal us from every wound;
Be about the beginning and end of our race,
Be giving us to sing in glory,
In peace, in rest, in reconciliation,
>    Where no tear shall be shed, where death
>        comes no more.
>    Where no tear shall be shed, where death
>        comes no more.

Alexander Carmichael[75]

### *Invocation*

God be in my head
and in my understanding.
God be in my eyes
and in my looking.
God be in my mouth
and in my speaking.
God be in my heart
and in my thinking.
God be at my end
and my departing.[76]

### For the Holy Women of Israel

Gracious God of love,
out of your overwhelming goodness,
you have chosen women in every age
to bear witness to your loving kindness.
By the example of those heroines of Israel,
Miriam, Ruth, Esther, and Judith;
of Mary, the mother of Jesus;
of Mary of Magdala;
and of all the female disciples
    and friends of Jesus,
raise up new women of strength,
mothers, sisters, martyrs, and mystics,
who will brave every adversity
in order to serve you faithfully,
for the benefit of us all.
In Jesus' name, we pray.
Amen.

### Hymn of Praise

This is a shorter, metrical version of the first section of
the *Te Deum*.

Holy God, we praise your name;
Lord of all, we bow before you;
All on earth your scepter claim,
All in heaven above adore you.
Infinite your vast domain,
Everlasting is your name.

Hark, the glad celestial hymn
Angel choirs above are raising;
Cherubim and seraphim,
In unceasing chorus praising,
Fill the heavens with sweet accord:
Holy, holy, holy Lord.

All apostles join the strain
As your sacred name they hallow;
Prophets swell the glad refrain,
And the blessed martyrs follow,
And from morn to set of sun,
Through the church the song goes on.

Holy Father, Holy Son,
Holy Spirit: Three we name you,
While in essence only One;
Undivided God we claim you,
And adoring bend the knee
While we own the mystery.[77]

### The Divine Praises

Blessed be God.
Blessed be his holy Name.
Blessed be Jesus Christ, true God and true man.
Blessed be the name of Jesus.
Blessed be his most Sacred Heart.
Blessed be his most Precious Blood.
Blessed be Jesus in the most holy Sacrament of the
    Altar.
Blessed be the Holy Spirit, the Paraclete.

Blessed be the great Mother of God, Mary most
    holy.
Blessed be her holy and Immaculate Conception.
Blessed be her glorious Assumption.
Blessed be the name of Mary, Virgin and Mother.
Blessed be St. Joseph, her most chaste spouse.
Blessed be God in his angels and in his saints.

### Doxology

Blessing and glory and wisdom
and thanksgiving and honor
and power and might
be to our God for ever and ever!
~Amen.

## Hymn to the Holy Spirit

Jesus' final gift to his disciples was the Holy Spirit, our
advocate and guide. The Spirit resides in our inmost
being as our comforter and consoler in good times and
bad. Come, Holy Spirit!

Creator Spirit, by whose aid
The world's foundations first were laid,
Come visit ev'ry pious mind;
Come pour thy joys on humankind:
From sin and sorrow set us free;
And make thy temples worthy thee.

O source of uncreated light,
The Father's promised *Paraclete*!
Thrice holy fount, thrice holy fire,
Our hearts with heav'nly love inspire;

Come, and thy sacred unction bring
To sanctify us, while we sing!

Plenteous of grace, descend from high,
Rich in thy sev'nfold energy!
Thou strength of his almighty hand,
Whose power does heaven and earth command:
Proceeding Spirit, our defense,
Who do'st the gift of tongues dispense,
And crown'st thy gift, with eloquence!

Refine and purge our earthly parts;
But, oh, inflame and fire our hearts!
Our frailties help, our vice control;
Submit the senses to the soul;
And when rebellious they are grown,
Then, lay thy hand, and hold 'em down.

Chase from our minds th' infernal foe;
And Peace, the fruit of love, bestow:
And, lest our feet should step astray,
Protect, and guide us in the way.

Make us eternal truths receive,
And practice, all that we believe:
Give us thyself, that we may see
The Father and the Son, by thee.

Immortal honor, endless fame
Attend th' almighty Father's name:
The savior Son, be glorified,
Who for lost man's redemption died:

And equal adoration be
Eternal *Paraclete* to thee.[78]

Send forth your Spirit, O Lord,
~AND RENEW THE FACE OF THE EARTH.

Let us pray for the gifts of the Spirit:

Come, Holy Spirit, come!
Come as holy fire and burn in us,
come as holy wind and cleanse us,
come as holy light and lead us,
come as holy truth and teach us,
come as holy forgiveness and free us,
come as holy love and enfold us,
come as holy power and enable us,
come as holy life and dwell in us,
convict us, convert us, consecrate us,
until we are wholly yours for your using
through Jesus Christ our Lord.
~AMEN.[79]

## *A Morning Prayer to the Holy Spirit*

O Holy and Astounding Spirit,
you catch me by surprise at least once a day
with the freshness of your love
and the unpredictability of your presence—
especially in humble things
that somehow give me immense joy.
Some moments are completely new, full of joy,
as uplifting as the dawning sun,

and those moments come from you,
    day by day.
Stand behind me today when I'm right
and ought to be more determined,
and block my way when I'm being stupid
and ought to back off.
Teach me true compassion for those in need,
so that I can be of genuine help to someone.
Bless me today, Holy Spirit, and astound me again!

Tom Noe[80]

### *A Prayer for Help*
Teach us, good Lord,
to serve you as you deserve;
to give and not count the cost;
to fight and not heed the wounds;
to toil and not seek for rest;
to labor and not ask for any reward,
except that of knowing that we do your will;
through Jesus Christ our Lord.
Amen.

Attributed to St. Ignatius Loyola (1491–1556)

# Praise from Scripture and the Saints

## *To Jesus*

Jesus of the Good News,
whose beauty is the joy of the heavenly host,
whose love inflames our love,
whose graciousness is our delight,
whose remembrance gives sweet light,
whose fragrance revives the dead:
Bring us at long last to the happiness
of all the saints of the heavenly Jerusalem,
for you are the brightness of eternal glory,
and the splendor of everlasting light,
now and always and for ever and ever.
~AMEN.

Adapted from St. Clare of Assisi (1194–1253)

## *The Canticle of the Church*

This hymn of praise is used in the Liturgy of the Hours
on most Sundays, on all major feasts, and on other
special occasions.

We praise you, O God,
we acclaim you as Lord;
all creation worships you,
the Father everlasting.

To you all angels, all the powers of heaven,
the cherubim and seraphim, sing in endless praise:
Holy, holy, holy Lord, God of power and might,
heaven and earth are full of your glory.

The glorious company of apostles praise you.
The noble fellowship of prophets praise you.
The white-robed army of martyrs praise you.

Throughout the world the holy church acclaims
you:
Father, of majesty unbounded,
your true and only Son, worthy of all praise,
the Holy Spirit, advocate and guide.

You, Christ, are the king of glory,
the eternal Son of the Father.
When you took our flesh to set us free
you humbly chose the Virgin's womb.

You overcame the sting of death
and opened the kingdom of heaven to all believers.
You are seated at God's right hand in glory.
We believe that you will come to be our judge.

Come, then, Lord and help your people,
bought with the price of your own blood,
and bring us with your saints
to glory everlasting.

St. Nicetas of Remesiana (ca. 335–ca. 414),
*Te Deum laudamus*

### The Canticle of All Creatures

St. Francis of Assisi (1181–1226) composed this song for his friars to sing as they carried the gospel across the world. The second-to-last stanza was probably composed after Francis had received the stigmata and was drawing near to his death. Let us rejoice with him in all God's creatures!

Most High, almighty, good Lord!
All praise, glory, honor, and exaltation are yours!
To you alone do they belong,
and no mere mortal dares pronounce your name.
~WE PRAISE YOU, O LORD!

Praise to you, O Lord our God, for all your
      creatures:
first, for our dear Brother Sun,
who gives us the day
and illumines us with his light;
fair is he, in splendor radiant,
bearing your very likeness, O Lord.
~WE PRAISE YOU, O LORD!

Praise to you for our Sister Moon,
and for the bright, shining stars:
~WE PRAISE YOU, O LORD!

Praise to you for our Brother Wind,
for fair and stormy seasons
and all heaven's varied moods,
by which you nourish all that you have made:
~WE PRAISE YOU, O LORD!

Praise to you for our Sister Water,
so useful, lowly, precious, and pure:
~We praise you, O Lord!

Praise to you for our Brother Fire,
who brightens up our darkest nights:
beautiful is he and eager,
invincible, and keen:
~We praise you, O Lord!

Praise to you for our dear Mother Earth,
who sustains and feeds us,
producing fair fruits,
and many-colored flowers and herbs:
~We praise you, O Lord!

Praise to you for those who forgive one another
        for love of you,
and who patiently bear sickness and other trials—
Happy are they who peacefully endure;
you will crown them, O Most High!
~We praise you, O Lord!

Praise to you for our Sister Death,
the inescapable fact of life—
Woe to those who die in mortal sin!
Happy are those she finds doing your will!
From the second death they stand immune:
~We praise you, O Lord!

All creatures
praise and glorify you, my Lord,

and give you thanks
and serve you in great humility:
~WE PRAISE YOU, O LORD!

**PRAYER**

Almighty, holy, high, and supreme God:
highest good, greatest good, and every good,
you who alone are good:
We give you all praise, all glory,
all thanksgiving, all honor, all blessing,
and we assign all good things to you.
Amen.

St. Francis of Assisi (1181–1226)[81]

## *Psalm 117: Act of Praise*

King David had a lot to be thankful for, and he was!
This is his shortest and pithiest psalm; let us join him
in praising and thanking God for all the blessings we
have received.

Holy, mighty, and deathless God, have mercy
on us.

Praise the Lord, all nations!
Extol the Lord, all peoples!

Holy, mighty, and deathless God, have mercy
on us.

Great is the Lord's steadfast love for us!
The faithfulness of the Lord endures for ever!

Holy, mighty, and deathless God, have mercy
on us.

Glory to the Father, and to the Son, and to the
Holy Spirit:
as it was in the beginning, is now, and will be
for ever. Amen.

Holy, mighty, and deathless God, have mercy
on us.

Psalm 117

**PRAYER**
Holy, mighty, and deathless God,
adored by the cherubim of many eyes,
worshipped by the fiery seraphim,
and praised by all the saints in glory:
Accept our humble praise and thanks,
and fresh prayers for all our needs,
for you are good and love humankind,
in and through Christ our Lord,
now and always and for ever and ever.
~AMEN.

## The Praises of God after Francis Received the Stigmata

Blessed Francis two years before his death kept a Lent in
the place of Mount La Verna in honor of the Blessed Virgin
Mary, the Mother of God, and of blessed Michael the
Archangel, from the Feast of the Assumption of the holy
Virgin Mary until the September Feast of Saint Michael.
And the hand of the Lord was laid upon him. After the
vision and the speech of the Seraph and the impression
of the Stigmata of Christ in his body, he composed these

praises . . . and wrote them in his own hand, giving
thanks to God for the benefits conferred upon him.

Brother Leo, his confessor, companion, and scribe

You are holy, Lord, the only God,
    and your deeds are wonderful.
You are strong.
    You are great.
    You are the Most High.
    You are almighty.
    You, Holy Father, are
    King of heaven and earth.
You are Three and One,
    Lord God, all good.
    You are Good, all Good, supreme Good,
    Lord God, living and true.
You are love,
    You are wisdom.
    You are humility,
    You are endurance.
    You are rest,
    You are peace.
    You are joy and gladness.
    You are justice and moderation.
    You are all our riches,
    And you suffice for us.
You are beauty.
    You are gentleness.
    You are our protector,
    You are our guardian and defender.

You are courage.
You are our haven and our hope.
You are our faith,
Our great consolation.
You are our eternal life,
Great and wonderful Lord,
God almighty,
Merciful Savior.

St. Francis of Assisi (1181–1226)[82]

## *Canticle of Moses*

This famous canticle sings of God's loving providence for Israel and of Israel's ingratitude. We can use these first few verses to encourage us to listen carefully to the gospel of Jesus and entrust us to his eagle wings that bear us up and keep us from falling.

Earth and sky hear my words,
listen closely to what I say.
My teaching will fall like drops of rain
and form on the earth like dew.
My words will fall like showers on young plants,
like gentle rain on tender grass.
I will praise the name of the Lord,
and his people will tell of his greatness.

The Lord is your mighty defender,
perfect and just in all his ways;
Your God is faithful and true;
he does what is right and fair.

Like an eagle teaching its young to fly,
catching them safely on its spreading wings,
the Lord kept Israel from falling.

Deuteronomy 32:1–4, 11, TEV

Let us pray for trust in our faithful God:

Most High God,
you founded a faithful covenant with ancient
    Israel
and put it into full force in Jesus.
Help us to heed his true words
and rely on the spreading wings of his cross
that protect us from the evil one
and keep us from falling into sin.
We ask this through Christ our Lord.
~Amen.

## A Canticle of King David

King David freely gave of his wealth and asked the ancestral leaders of Israel to do the same so that his son Solomon could build a gorgeous temple in honor of God. Impressed by their generosity, David blessed the Lord in the presence of the great assembly of the people. When we come to sense what the people of God do so generously for the church and the world, we can use David's words for our purposes.

Blessed are you, O Lord,
the God of our ancestors,
for ever and ever.

Yours, O LORD, are the greatness, the power,
the glory, the victory, and the majesty;
for all that is in the heavens and on the earth is
      yours;

Yours is the kingdom, O LORD,
and you are exalted as head above all.
Riches and honor come from you,
and you rule over all.

In your hand are power and might;
and it is in your hand to make great
and to give strength to all.

And now, our God, we give thanks to you
and praise your glorious name.

1 Chronicles 29:10–13

Glory to the Holy and Undivided Trinity:
now and always, and for ever and ever. Amen.

Let us pray for generosity:

May royal David's prayer
inspire us to generous giving
and exuberant celebrations of the liturgy
that urge us to fuller acknowledgment
of God's glorious name.
For Jesus' sake we ask it.
~AMEN.

### Canticle of Tobit
Wherever we are in this world, we find ourselves part of
God's plan to spread the gospel in our neighborhood,

city, school, country, and the world. We are personally called to make God's greatness known.

Blessed be God who lives for ever,
blessed be God who rules over all.
We give thanks to you, O Lord, before the nations,
for you have scattered us among them.
There we make your greatness known
and exalt you in the presence of all the living,
because you are the Lord our God;
you are our Father for ever.

Tobit 13:1, 3–4

Let us pray for the universal church:

Ruler of the nations,
you place us among the nations of the world
to spread your name and gospel
for everybody's benefit.
Give us the grace to exemplify your teaching
and to exalt you in the presence of all the living.
We ask this through Christ our Lord.
~AMEN.

### *A Canticle of Judith*
Judith was a heroine of Israel who scattered the Assyrian army and saved her people from slavery. She was a foreshadowing of the Virgin Mary who bore our blessed Savior. Let us rejoice in the victory of these heroic women and put our trust in the same God who gave them courage and strength in their time of need.

Strike up the instruments,
a song to my God with timbrels,
chant to the Lord with cymbals;
Sing to him a new song,
exalt and acclaim his name.

For the Lord is God; he crushes warfare,
and sets his encampment among his people;
he snatched me from the hands of my persecutors.
But the Lord Almighty thwarted them,
by a woman's hand he confounded them.

Judith 16:1–2, 5, NAB

Let us pray for deliverance from our enemies:

May the heroines of Israel, O God,
inspire us with faith and trust
so that we can overcome all our enemies,
seen and unseen, and, by your gift,
become your chosen instruments of salvation.
We ask this through Christ our Lord.
~Amen.

### *The Righteous in the Sight of God*

The righteous live forever,
and their reward is with the Lord;
the Most High takes care of them.
Therefore they will receive a glorious crown
and a beautiful diadem from the hand of the Lord,
because with his right hand he will cover them,
and with his arm he will shield them.

Wisdom 5:15–16

Let us pray for God-given holiness:

We are righteous in your sight, O God,
because you have chosen us in your dear Son
and filled us with his holy teaching
and his rejuvenating grace.
Thank you for your promise of protection
and of reward after a life of faithfulness.
Blest be the Savior of the world.
~AMEN.

## A Prayer for Wisdom

Wisdom is a taste for God and his revelation in his
blessed Son Jesus who is always near at hand and
ready to help.

Wisdom is radiant and unfading,
and she is easily discerned
    by those who love her,
and is found by those who seek her.
She hastens to make herself known
    to those who desire her.

One who rises early to seek her
    will have no difficulty,
for she will be found sitting at the gate.
To fix one's thought on her
    is perfect understanding,
and one who is vigilant on her account
    will soon be free from care,
because she goes about seeking
    those worthy of her,

and she graciously appears to them
in their paths,
and meets them in every thought.

Wisdom 6:12–16; 9:1–4

### *Prayer of Wise Solomon*

O God of my ancestors and Lord of mercy,
who have made all things by your word,
and by your wisdom have formed humankind
to have dominion over the creatures you have
made,
and rule the world in holiness and righteousness,
and pronounce judgment in uprightness of soul,
give me the wisdom that sits by your throne,
and do not reject me from among your servants.
~AMEN.

### *Our Messiah and Lord*

In virtue of the incarnation of the Word of God, we are elevated by faith in Jesus to a new dignity and confidence in the plan of God for us. He was indeed born for us and died and rose for us, to give us a fresh status in grace and in truth.

The people who walked in darkness
have seen a great light;
those who lived in a land of deep darkness—
on them light has shined.
For a child has been born for us,
a son given to us;
authority rests upon his shoulders;

and he is named
Wonderful Counselor, Mighty God,
Everlasting Father, Prince of Peace.

His authority shall grow continually,
and there shall be endless peace
for the throne of David and his kingdom.

Isaiah 9:2, 6–7

The Word was made flesh, alleluia!
~AND DWELT AMONG US, ALLELUIA!

**PRAYER**
God and Father,
we thank you for creating us
and still more for restoring us
in the incarnation of your blessed Son.
May the Prince of Peace
bring us into the land of glory.
He is our Savior, now and for ever.
~AMEN.

## God Is My Salvation
God is our mighty rescuer, deliverer, Savior. Our job is
to trust in God, the mighty and the merciful.

Surely God is my salvation;
I will trust, and will not be afraid,
for the LORD GOD is my strength
and my might;
he has become my salvation.

Isaiah 12:2

You shall call his name Jesus
~For he will save his people from their sins.

PRAYER
Lord Jesus Christ,
your holy Father entrusted us to you,
making you our Savior at all times.
Jesus is your name
so be Jesus for us, now and for ever.
~Amen.

## *The Prince of Peace*
We know that we are surrounded by enemies in this
life. And even without paranoia, we know that they are
out to get us. In God we trust!

O Lord, you will ordain peace for us,
for indeed, all that we have done,
you have done for us.
O Lord our God, other lords besides you
    have ruled over us,
but we acknowledge your name alone.

Isaiah 26:12–13

Peace be within our walls,
~And security within our towers.

PRAYER
Mighty God,
author of peace and lover of concord,
to know you is life eternal

and to serve you perfect freedom:
Defend us against our enemies,
bodily and spiritual,
that, trusting in your strength,
we may not have any foe to fear.
We ask this through Christ our Lord.
~Amen.

### Our Incomparable God

We all grow weary from time to time—old folks especially, and even youth. But the Creator does not grow weary or exhausted. He helps us rise on eagles' wings!

The Lord is the everlasting God,
the Creator of the ends of the earth.
He does not faint or grow weary;
his understanding is unsearchable.

He gives power to the faint,
and strengthens the powerless.
Even youths will faint and be weary,
and the young will fall exhausted;
but those who wait for the Lord
shall renew their strength,
they shall mount up with wings like eagles,
they shall run and not be weary,
they shall walk and not faint.

Isaiah 40:28–31

## PRAYER

Everlasting and powerful God,
we must trust in you and your strength
for you are never tired or exhausted.
May we rely on you when life wearies us
and take fresh inspiration from you
as we need it.
Blessed be our God, now and for ever.
~Amen.

## *God's Servant*

God promises us support and encouragement through his servant Jesus who fulfilled the prophecy of Isaiah (see Matthew 12:15–21).

Here is my servant, whom I uphold,
my chosen, in whom my soul delights;
I have put my spirit upon him;
he will bring forth justice to the nations.
He will not cry or lift up his voice,
or make it heard in the street;
a bruised reed he will not break,
and a dimly burning wick
   he will not quench;
he will faithfully bring forth justice.
He will not grow faint or be crushed
until he has established justice in the earth;
and the coastlands wait for his teaching.

Isaiah 42:1–4

Holy Father,
you sent your only and dear Son
to be the tireless creator of justice for your people.
May Jesus who cherishes us
and never treats us harshly
or discourages us,
be our hope and promise while we await
the coming of his reign of justice and peace.
We ask this through the same Christ our Lord.
~AMEN.

## God's Promise

Whenever we think all is darkness in our base world,
let us remember the great prophets like Isaiah and their
promise of Jesus, the Light of the world.

Arise, shine, for your light has come,
and the glory of the LORD has risen upon you.
Behold, darkness covers the earth
and thick darkness is over the peoples.
But upon you the Lord shall rise
and the glory of the Lord will appear upon you.
Nations will come to your light
and kings to the brightness of your rising.
No longer will violence be heard in your land
nor ruin of destruction within your borders.
But you will call your walls "Salvation"
and all your gates "Praise."

Isaiah 60:1–3, 17–18

Let us pray for the glory of the Lord:

Glorious God,
your dear Jesus is the Light of the world
even when darkness seems to reign
in every nook and cranny of our fallen condition.
May he rise and shine upon us
and be your bright light
for all the nations and peoples of the earth;
now and always, and for ever and ever.
~AMEN.

### The Great Transit
Lord Jesus Christ,
from the bosom of the Father
you descended into the womb of the Virgin,
from the womb you visited the cradle,
from the cradle you came to the cross,
from the cross to the tomb,
from the tomb you arose in glory
and ascended into heaven:
By this great transit of mercy—
you becoming as we are
and we becoming as you are—
grant us, O Savior of the world,
the fullness of our divine adoption
as sons and daughters of the living God.
You live and reign, now and for ever.
~AMEN.[83]

# IV
# Invocations,
# Litanies, and
# Prayers in Special
# Seasons

## Prayers in Special Seasons

### Prayer in Advent
This season of the church year is one of waiting and expectancy. We recollect and celebrate the first coming of Jesus into the world for our salvation, and we look forward with supreme confidence to his second coming in glory at the end of time. We put our hope in both comings because he did what he could for us in the first coming and has solemnly promised to accomplish his work when he comes again. Come, Lord Jesus! Come!

#### ANTIPHON
In the wilderness prepare the way of the LORD, make straight in the desert a highway for our God.

The glory of the LORD shall be revealed,
and all people shall see it together,
for the mouth of the LORD has spoken.

Isaiah 40:3, 5

Every valley shall be lifted up,
~AND EVERY MOUNTAIN AND HILL BE MADE LOW.

**PRAYER**
Lord and Comforter of your people,
inspired by the first coming of Jesus
and awaiting his second coming,
we look forward to your mighty help
when we feel distressed and oppressed.
We put our trust in Jesus, our healer and rescuer,
who felt compassion for the human race
and worked with all his strength for us
while he was on earth.
Now he intercedes for us unceasingly
as he stands as our great high priest
at the right hand of God his Father.
Hear our prayers, O Lord, . . .
and deliver us from all that disheartens us
and prepare us for the Second Coming in glory.
We ask this in Jesus' name.
~AMEN.

## *Prayer in Christmastide*
Christmas is the season of holy rejoicing in Jesus the
Messiah who was born for us of the Virgin Mary in the
stable of Bethlehem. Upon his birth, the Christ child

was glorified in three ways: the choir of angels sang, "Glory to God in the highest and peace to God's people on earth"; the shepherds of Bethlehem "made known what had been told them about this Child"; and "Mary treasured all these words and pondered them in her heart" (Luke 2:13–20). Let us join them in our rejoicing at what God has done—and is doing—for us.

## ANTIPHON

A child has been born for us,
a son given to us; and he is named
Wonderful Counselor, Mighty God,
Everlasting Father, Prince of Peace.

Isaiah 9:6

His authority shall grow continually,
~AND THERE SHALL BE ENDLESS PEACE.

## PRAYER

Gracious God and Father,
you cradled your dear Son
in the arms of the Virgin Mary
and her lap became a throne
for divine wisdom.
As we regard this holy scene,
lift our hearts to you in all confidence,
recalling that Jesus is Emmanuel,
God-is-with-us, unfailingly.
Hear our prayers, good Lord, . . .
and deliver us from all that depresses us.
In Jesus' name we ask it.
~AMEN.

### *Prayer in Lent*

This is the season of preparation for those who will be baptized at Easter and for those seeking to repent of post-baptismal sin. God is good and Jesus is our Savior, now and always and for ever and ever! Let us renew our baptismal vows to the faithful Lord who cares for us.

### *Hymn of St. Patrick*

Christ be here at either hand,
Christ behind, before me stand,
Christ with me where'er I go,
Christ around, above, below.

Christ be in my heart and mind,
Christ within my soul enshrined,
Christ control my wayward heart,
Christ abide and ne'er depart.

Christ my life and only way,
Christ my lantern night and day,
Christ be my unchanging friend,
Guide and shepherd to the end.

~Amen

#### Antiphon

Wash yourselves; make yourselves clean;
remove the evil of your doings from before my
      eyes;
cease to do evil, learn to do good;
seek justice, rescue the oppressed,
defend the orphan, plead for the widow.

Isaiah 1:16–17

The kingdom of God has come near;
~Repent, and believe in the good news.

## Prayer
Merciful Father of us all,
through Isaiah the Prophet you promised
that "though our sins are like scarlet,
they shall be like snow;
though they are red like crimson,
they shall become like wool."
As we remember our sins and failings,
give us trusting and penitent hearts
in your unbroken promises of forgiveness.
By the precious blood of Jesus
shed on the hill of Golgotha,
wash us clean of all our offenses,
and make us your loving and obedient children,
now and for ever.
~Amen.

## Prayer in Holy Week
The high holy days of our religion fall between Palm Sunday and Easter Sunday. Jesus enters the holy city of Jerusalem in triumph, celebrates the sacrament of love with his disciples, dies on the cross of pain, descends to the netherworld to rescue our holy forebears, and gloriously rises on the third day. What more could our Savior do for us?

## Hymn
All you who seek a comfort sure
In trouble and distress,

Whatever sorrow vex the mind,
Or guilt the soul oppress,
Jesus who gave himself for you
Upon the cross to die,
Opens to you his sacred heart;
Oh, to that heart draw nigh.

You hear how kindly he invites;
You hear his words so blest:
"All you that labor come to me,
And I will give you rest."
Christ Jesus, joy of saints on high,
The hope of sinners here,
Attracted by those loving words
To you we lift our prayer.

Edward Caswall (1814–1878)

**ANTIPHON**
Jesus emptied himself, taking the form of a slave,
being born in human likeness.
And being found in human form,
he humbled himself
and became obedient to the point of death—
even death on a cross.

Philippians 2:7–8

Every tongue should confess
~THAT JESUS CHRIST IS LORD.

## Prayer

Lord Jesus Christ,
Son of the living God,
you handed yourself over to sinners
and were nailed to the cross for our salvation.
By your five precious wounds,
deliver us from all sin and sorrow
and make us stand at your side,
confessing your lordship,
for ever and ever.
~Amen.

### Prayer in Eastertide

"We are Easter people and alleluia is our song"
(St. Augustine of Hippo Regius).

God raised Christ from the dead and vindicated his person and his teaching before the world. He is the firstfruits of those who have died and the bringer of eternal life to all who trust in him. In hope and trust we find our best response to the Easter event.

### The Coronation Hymn

All hail the power of Jesus' name;
Let angels prostrate fall;
Bring forth the royal diadem
And crown him Lord of all.

Crown him, you martyrs of our God,
Who from his altar call;
Extol the flower of Jesse's rod,
And crown him Lord of all.

You chosen saints of Israel's race
Now ransomed from the fall,
Hail Christ who saves you by his grace
And crown him Lord of all.

Let every nation, every tongue
Before him prostrate fall,
And shout in universal song
To Christ the Lord of all.

Edward Perronet (1726–1792)[89]

## Antiphon

God so loved the world that he gave his only Son,
so that everyone who believes in him may not
     perish but may have eternal life.
Indeed, God did not send the Son into the world
to condemn the world,
but in order that the world might be saved
     through him.

John 3:16–17

We adore your cross, O Lord, alleluia!
~AND WE GLORIFY YOUR HOLY RESURRECTION,
    ALLELUIA!

## Prayer

Abba, dear Father,
you lifted your dear Son from the grave
and made him a beacon of hope for all mortals.
By overcoming sin and death and hell,
may he take us by the hand

and conduct us into the land of bliss and glory
where we shall enjoy for ever
the company of the whole heavenly host.
May we trust with all our hearts in his glorious
	wounds
by which he ransomed us for everlasting life.
Blessed be the name of Jesus, now and for ever.
~AMEN.

# Special Invocations

## To the Blessed Trinity

ANTIPHON The Father is my hope.
The Son is my refuge.
The Holy Spirit is my protector.
Glory to the Holy and Undivided Trinity, now and
	for ever.

Let us praise the Father, the Son, and the Holy
	and Life-giving Spirit;
~LET US BLESS AND EXALT GOD ABOVE ALL FOR
	EVER.

Let us pray:

God, we praise you:
Father all powerful, Christ Lord and Savior, Spirit
	of love.
You reveal yourself in the depths of our being,
drawing us to share in your life and your love.
One God, three Persons,

be near to the people formed in your image,
close to the world your love brings to life.
We ask this, Father, Son, and Holy Spirit,
one God, true and living, for ever and ever.
~Amen.[84]

## To the Holy Spirit

ANTIPHON Come, Holy Spirit, fill the hearts
of your faithful and kindle in them the fire of
your love.

When you send forth your Spirit, they are created;
~AND YOU RENEW THE FACE OF THE EARTH.
Psalm 104:30

Let us pray:

Almighty and everlasting God,
you teach the minds and hearts
of those who believe in you
by the light of the Holy Spirit:
Under the inspiration of that same Spirit,
fill us with the precious gifts and fruits of the
Spirit
that Jesus promised us,
and conduct us into the freedom of the children
of God.
We ask this through the same Christ our Lord.
~Amen.

## Prayer to the Holy Spirit

Heavenly Ruler, Consoler, Spirit of truth,

present in all places and filling all things,
treasury of blessings and giver of life:
Come and dwell in us,
cleanse us from every stain of sin,
and save our souls,
O gracious Lord.
~Amen.[85]

## To the Sacred Heart of Jesus
**Antiphon**

God is love, and those who abide in love
abide in God and God in them, alleluia!

1 John 4:16

Come to me all you who are burdened
~And I will give you rest.

Let us pray:

Father,
we have wounded the heart of Jesus your Son,
but he brings us forgiveness and grace.
Help us to prove our grateful love
and make amends for our sins.
We ask this through our Lord Jesus Christ, your
    Son,
who lives and reigns with you,
in the unity of the Holy Spirit,
one God, for ever and ever.
~Amen.[86]

### Prayer before a Crucifix

Good and gentle Jesus,
I kneel before you.
I see and ponder your five wounds.
My eyes behold what David prophesied about you:
"They have pierced my hands and feet;
They have counted all my bones."

Engrave on me this image of yourself.
Fulfill the yearnings of my heart:
give me faith, hope, and love,
repentance for my sins,
and true conversion of life.
~Amen.[87]

### The Precious Blood of Jesus

Precious Blood,
Ocean of Divine Mercy:
Flow upon us!

Precious Blood,
Most pure Offering:
Procure us every grace!

Precious Blood,
Hope and Refuge of sinners:
Atone for us!

Precious Blood,
Delight of holy souls:
Draw us!
Amen.

St. Catherine of Siena (1347–1380)[88]

### In Honor of the Holy Cross

**ANTIPHON** Jesus, the Lord of glory was crucified
by the rulers of this age for the salvation of the
world.

Proclaim to the nations:
~THE LORD REIGNS FROM THE TREE OF THE
CROSS.

Let us pray:

Righteous God,
when Jesus cried out to you on the cross,
you rescued him from the power of the grave
and made him the Savior of the world.
By his pierced and bleeding wounds,
wash away our sins in the blood and water
that poured from his Sacred Heart
and bring us to new life in the Spirit.
We ask this through the same Christ our Lord,
who lives and reigns with you,
in the unity of the Holy Spirit,
one God, for ever and ever.
~AMEN.

### To St. John the Baptist, Jesus' Forerunner

**ANTIPHON** There was a man sent from God
whose name was John. He came to bear witness to
the Light,
to prepare an upright people for the Lord.

There is no one born of woman
~GREATER THAN JOHN THE BAPTIST.

Let us pray for true repentance:

God our Father,
the voice of John the Forerunner
challenges us to repentance
and points the way to Christ our Lord.
Open our ears to his message
and turn our hearts to the Good News
proclaimed by Christ himself.
His reign is a reign for all ages.
~AMEN.

## To Michael the Archangel, Prince of the Heavenly Host

**ANTIPHON** War broke out in heaven; Michael and
his angels fought against the dragon. The dragon
and his angels fought back, but they were defeated,
alleluia!

Revelation 12:7–8

The ancient serpent who is called the devil and
    Satan,
~THE DECEIVER OF THE WHOLE WORLD WAS
    THROWN DOWN.

Let us pray to St. Michael, the prince of the
    heavenly host:

Holy Michael the Archangel,
defend us in the day of battle.

Be our safeguard against the wickedness
and snares of the devil.
May God rebuke him, we humbly pray,
and do you, O prince of the heavenly host,
   by the power of God,
thrust down to hell Satan and all the wicked
      spirits
who wander about the world seeking the ruin of
      souls.
~AMEN.

Pope Leo XIII (1878-1903)

### TO ST. JOSEPH, PATRON OF THE DYING

ANTIPHON The just shall flourish like the palm
tree, shall grow like the cedar of Lebanon. Planted
in the house of the LORD, they shall flourish in the
courts of our God.

Psalm 92:12–14

They shall bear fruit even in old age
~ALWAYS VIGOROUS AND STURDY.

Let us pray to good St. Joseph:

Blessed God,
you raised up St. Joseph
to be the guide and guardian of the holy family.
By your help and example,
may we lead a holy life, die a godly death,
and attain to a blessed eternity in heaven.
We ask this through Christ our Lord.
~AMEN.

### To Padre Pio of Pietralcina

(1887–1968; canonized, 2002)

**ANTIPHON** I have been crucified with Christ; and it is no longer I who live, but it is Christ who lives in me.

Galatians 2:19–20

The life I now live in the flesh
~I LIVE BY FAITH IN THE SON OF GOD.

Let us pray for cross-centered piety:

Lord Jesus Crucified,
you imprinted your five precious wounds
in the soul and body of your priest Pio
who served you faithfully and heroically
for a long lifetime of patient suffering.
By his example and prayers,
warm our cold hearts
and make us fervent disciples of the cross
by which you saved the world.
Your reign is a reign for all ages.
~AMEN.

### To Mother Teresa of Calcutta

(1910–1997; beatified, October 19, 2003)

**ANTIPHON** I give you a new commandment , that you love one another. Just as I have loved you, you also should love one another.

John 13:34

By this everyone will know
~THAT YOU ARE MY DISCIPLES.

Let us pray:

God of love and compassion,
you raised up Mother Teresa
to serve the dying and abandoned
with perfect charity.
By her example and prayers,
bless the two religious orders she founded,
help them do something beautiful for God,
and make her a model of Christian life and service
for all who desire to walk in her footsteps.
We ask this in Jesus' name.
~AMEN.

### To Dorothy Day

(1897–1980; cofounder of the *Catholic Worker*)

**ANTIPHON** Let us look to Jesus the pioneer and
perfecter of our faith, who for the sake of the
joy that was set before him endured the cross,
disregarding its shame.

Hebrews 12:2

In the cross is victory, alleluia!
~IN THE CROSS IS POWER, ALLELUIA!

Let us pray for perfect charity:

Lord Jesus Messiah,
in the shadow of two world wars
and the age of the atom bomb,

you raised up Dorothy Day to inspire us
with a fresh understanding of the Sermon on the
    Mount
and of the reconciling Lord who preached it to us.
May her prayers accompany us on our journey
to the land of peace and plenty
where you bring us all together
under the arms of your cross
that heals all our wounds.
Blessed be your holy Name, now and for ever.
~AMEN.

# Litanies of Intercession

Litanies are forms of intercessory prayer appropriate to our condition. Their prayerful rhythm echoes the wonderful attributes of our Savior and his mother while their lyrics fill our hearts with beautiful phrases of spiritual longing and power. Litanies draw us into our Father's loving embrace and concentrate our minds and hearts on asking for what we need. Because of their repetitive petition-answer format, litanies are particularly helpful as part of a novena of intercession or thanksgiving in a family or other group.

> Ask, and it will be given you;
> Search, and you will find;
> Knock, and the door will be opened for you.
>
> Matthew 7:7

## *Litany of the Holy Name of Jesus*

| | |
|---|---|
| Lord, have mercy. | ~LORD HAVE MERCY. |
| Christ, have mercy. | ~CHRIST, HAVE MERCY. |
| Lord, have mercy. | ~LORD HAVE MERCY. |
| God the Father in heaven, | ~HAVE MERCY ON US. |
| God the Son, Redeemer of the world, | ~HAVE MERCY ON US. |
| God the Holy Spirit, | ~HAVE MERCY ON US. |
| Holy Trinity, one God, | ~HAVE MERCY ON US. |
| Jesus, Son of the living God, | ~HAVE MERCY ON US. |
| Jesus, splendor of the Father, | ~HAVE MERCY ON US. |
| Jesus, brightness of everlasting light, | ~HAVE MERCY ON US. |
| Jesus, king of glory, | ~HAVE MERCY ON US. |
| Jesus, dawn of justice, | ~HAVE MERCY ON US. |
| Jesus, Son of the Virgin Mary, | ~HAVE MERCY ON US. |
| Jesus, worthy of our love, | ~HAVE MERCY ON US. |

| | |
|---|---|
| Jesus, worthy of our wonder, | ~HAVE MERCY ON US. |
| Jesus, mighty God, | ~HAVE MERCY ON US. |
| Jesus, father of the world to come, | ~HAVE MERCY ON US. |
| Jesus, prince of peace, | ~HAVE MERCY ON US. |
| Jesus, all powerful, | ~HAVE MERCY ON US. |
| Jesus, pattern of patience, | ~HAVE MERCY ON US. |
| Jesus, model of obedience, | ~HAVE MERCY ON US. |
| Jesus, gentle and humble of heart, | ~HAVE MERCY ON US. |
| Jesus, lover of chastity, | ~HAVE MERCY ON US. |
| Jesus, lover of us all, | ~HAVE MERCY ON US. |
| Jesus, God of peace, | ~HAVE MERCY ON US. |
| Jesus, author of life, | ~HAVE MERCY ON US. |
| Jesus, model of goodness, | ~HAVE MERCY ON US. |
| Jesus, seeker of souls, | ~HAVE MERCY ON US. |
| Jesus, our God, | ~HAVE MERCY ON US. |
| Jesus, our refuge, | ~HAVE MERCY ON US. |
| Jesus, father of the poor, | ~HAVE MERCY ON US. |
| Jesus, treasure of the faithful, | ~HAVE MERCY ON US. |
| Jesus, Good Shepherd, | ~HAVE MERCY ON US. |
| Jesus, true light, | ~HAVE MERCY ON US. |
| Jesus, eternal wisdom, | ~HAVE MERCY ON US. |
| Jesus, infinite goodness, | ~HAVE MERCY ON US. |
| Jesus, our way and our life, | ~HAVE MERCY ON US. |
| Jesus, joy of angels, | ~HAVE MERCY ON US. |
| Jesus, king of patriarchs, | ~HAVE MERCY ON US. |
| Jesus, teacher of apostles, | ~HAVE MERCY ON US. |
| Jesus, master of evangelists, | ~HAVE MERCY ON US. |
| Jesus, courage of martyrs, | ~HAVE MERCY ON US. |
| Jesus, light of confessors, | ~HAVE MERCY ON US. |
| Jesus, purity of virgins, | ~HAVE MERCY ON US. |
| Jesus, crown of all saints, | ~HAVE MERCY ON US. |
| Lord, be merciful, | ~JESUS, SAVE YOUR PEOPLE. |
| From all evil, | ~JESUS, SAVE YOUR PEOPLE. |

| | |
|---|---|
| From every sin, | ~JESUS, SAVE YOUR PEOPLE. |
| From the snares of the devil, | ~JESUS, SAVE YOUR PEOPLE. |
| From your anger, | ~JESUS, SAVE YOUR PEOPLE. |
| From the spirit of infidelity, | ~JESUS, SAVE YOUR PEOPLE. |
| From everlasting death, | ~JESUS, SAVE YOUR PEOPLE. |
| From neglect of your Holy Spirit, | ~JESUS, SAVE YOUR PEOPLE. |
| By the mystery of your incarnation, | ~JESUS, SAVE YOUR PEOPLE. |
| By your birth, | ~JESUS, SAVE YOUR PEOPLE. |
| By your childhood, | ~JESUS, SAVE YOUR PEOPLE. |
| By your hidden life, | ~JESUS, SAVE YOUR PEOPLE. |
| By your public ministry, | ~JESUS, SAVE YOUR PEOPLE. |
| By your agony and crucifixion, | ~JESUS, SAVE YOUR PEOPLE. |
| By your abandonment, | ~JESUS, SAVE YOUR PEOPLE. |
| By your grief and sorrow, | ~JESUS, SAVE YOUR PEOPLE. |
| By your death and burial, | ~JESUS, SAVE YOUR PEOPLE. |
| By your rising to new life, | ~JESUS, SAVE YOUR PEOPLE. |
| By your return in glory to the Father, | ~JESUS, SAVE YOUR PEOPLE. |
| By your gift of the holy eucharist, | ~JESUS, SAVE YOUR PEOPLE. |
| By your joy and glory, | ~JESUS, SAVE YOUR PEOPLE. |
| Christ, hear us. | ~CHRIST, HEAR US. |
| Lord Jesus, hear our prayer. | ~LORD JESUS, HEAR OUR PRAYER. |
| Lamb of God, you take away the sins of the world, | ~HAVE MERCY ON US. |
| Lamb of God, you take away the sins of the world, | ~HAVE MERCY ON US. |
| Lamb of God, you take away the sins of the world, | ~HAVE MERCY ON US. |

Litanies of Intersession **207**

Let us pray:

Lord, may we who honor the holy name of Jesus,
enjoy his friendship in this life
and be filled with eternal joy in the kingdom
where he lives and reigns for ever and ever.
~AMEN.[90]

## *Litany of the Sacred Heart of Jesus*

| | |
|---|---|
| Lord, have mercy. | ~LORD, HAVE MERCY. |
| Christ, have mercy. | ~CHRIST, HAVE MERCY. |
| Lord, have mercy. | ~LORD, HAVE MERCY. |
| God our Father in heaven, | ~HAVE MERCY ON US. |
| God the Son,<br>    Redeemer of the world, | ~HAVE MERCY ON US. |
| God the Holy Spirit, | ~HAVE MERCY ON US. |
| Holy Trinity, one God, | ~HAVE MERCY ON US. |
| Heart of Jesus, Son of the eternal<br>    Father, | ~HAVE MERCY ON US. |
| Heart of Jesus, formed by the<br>    Holy Spirit<br>    in the womb of the Virgin<br>    Mother, | ~HAVE MERCY ON US. |
| Heart of Jesus, one with the<br>    eternal Word, | ~HAVE MERCY ON US. |
| Heart of Jesus, infinite in majesty, | ~HAVE MERCY ON US. |
| Heart of Jesus, holy temple of God | ~HAVE MERCY ON US. |
| Heart of Jesus, tabernacle of the<br>    Most High, | ~HAVE MERCY ON US. |
| Heart of Jesus, house of God and<br>    gate of heaven, | ~HAVE MERCY ON US. |
| Heart of Jesus, aflame with love<br>    for us, | ~HAVE MERCY ON US. |

Heart of Jesus, source of justice
and love, ~HAVE MERCY ON US.

Heart of Jesus, full of goodness
and love, ~HAVE MERCY ON US.

Heart of Jesus, wellspring of all
virtue, ~HAVE MERCY ON US.

Heart of Jesus, worthy of all praise, ~HAVE MERCY ON US.

Heart of Jesus, king and center of
all hearts, ~HAVE MERCY ON US.

Heart of Jesus, treasure-house of
wisdom and knowledge, ~HAVE MERCY ON US.

Heart of Jesus, in whom there
dwells the fullness of God, ~HAVE MERCY ON US.

Heart of Jesus, in whom the Father
is well pleased, ~HAVE MERCY ON US.

Heart of Jesus, of whose fullness
we have all received, ~HAVE MERCY ON US.

Heart of Jesus, desire of the
everlasting hills, ~HAVE MERCY ON US.

Heart of Jesus, patient and full
of mercy, ~HAVE MERCY ON US.

Heart of Jesus, generous to all who
turn to you, ~HAVE MERCY ON US.

Heart of Jesus, fountain of life and
holiness, ~HAVE MERCY ON US.

Heart of Jesus, atonement for our
sins, ~HAVE MERCY ON US.

Heart of Jesus, overwhelmed
with insults, ~HAVE MERCY ON US.

Heart of Jesus, broken for our sins, ~HAVE MERCY ON US.

Heart of Jesus, obedient even to
death, ~HAVE MERCY ON US.

Heart of Jesus, pierced by a lance, ~HAVE MERCY ON US.

Heart of Jesus, source of all
consolation, ~HAVE MERCY ON US.

Heart of Jesus, our life and
  resurrection,                    ~HAVE MERCY ON US.
Heart of Jesus, our peace and
  reconciliation,                  ~HAVE MERCY ON US.
Heart of Jesus, victim for our sins,   ~HAVE MERCY ON US.
Heart of Jesus, salvation of all
  who trust in you,                ~HAVE MERCY ON US.
Heart of Jesus, hope of all who
  die in you,                      ~HAVE MERCY ON US.
Heart of Jesus, delight of all the
  saints,                          ~HAVE MERCY ON US.

Lamb of God, you take away the
  sins of the world,               ~HAVE MERCY ON US.
Lamb of God, you take away the
  sins of the world,               ~HAVE MERCY ON US.
Lamb of God, you take away the
  sins of the world,               ~HAVE MERCY ON US.

Jesus, gentle and            ~TOUCH OUR HEARTS AND
humble of heart,          MAKE THEM LIKE YOUR OWN.

Let us pray:

Father,
we rejoice in the gifts of love
we have received from the heart of Jesus your Son.
Open our hearts to share his life
and continue to bless us with his love.
We ask this in the name of Jesus the Lord.
~AMEN.[91]

## Litany of the Resurrection

In peace, let us pray to the Lord.     ~LORD, HAVE MERCY.

For peace from on high, and for the salvation of our souls,
  let us pray to the Lord.              ~LORD, HAVE MERCY.

That the Lord Jesus Christ, our Savior, may grant us triumph and victory over the temptations of our visible and invisible enemies,

let us pray to the Lord. ~LORD, HAVE MERCY.

That He* may crush beneath our feet the prince of darkness and his powers,

let us pray to the Lord. ~LORD, HAVE MERCY.

That He may raise us up with Him, and make us rise from the tomb of our sins and offenses,

let us pray to the Lord. ~LORD, HAVE MERCY.

That He may purify us, and make us shine with the glory of His holy resurrection,

let us pray to the Lord. ~LORD, HAVE MERCY.

That we may deserve the grace of entering into the chamber of his divine wedding feast, and to rejoice beyond words, together with His heavenly attendants and the hosts of the saints glorified through Him in the Church Triumphant,

let us pray to the Lord. ~LORD, HAVE MERCY.

That we may be delivered from all affliction, wrath, danger, and need,

let us pray to the Lord. ~LORD, HAVE MERCY.

Help us, save us, have mercy on us, and protect us, O God, by your grace. ~LORD, HAVE MERCY.

Let us remember the all-holy, spotless, most highly blessed, and glorious Lady, the mother of God and ever-Virgin Mary, and all the saints, and commend ourselves, one another, and our whole life to Christ our God.

~TO YOU, O LORD.

For You are our Light and our Resurrection, O Christ God; and we send up glory to You, and to Your eternal

Father, and to Your all-holy, good, and life-giving
Spirit, now and always, and for ever and ever.
~AMEN.[92]

## *Litany of the Blessed Sacrament*

| | |
|---|---|
| Lord, have mercy. | ~LORD, HAVE MERCY. |
| Christ, have mercy. | ~CHRIST, HAVE MERCY. |
| Lord, have mercy. | ~LORD, HAVE MERCY. |
| God our Father in heaven, | ~HAVE MERCY ON US. |
| God the Son, Redeemer of the world, | ~HAVE MERCY ON US. |
| God the Holy Spirit, | ~HAVE MERCY ON US. |
| Holy Trinity, one God, | ~HAVE MERCY ON US. |
| Word made flesh and living among us, | ~CHRIST, HAVE MERCY ON US. |
| Pure and acceptable sacrifice, | ~CHRIST, HAVE MERCY ON US. |
| Hidden manna from above, | ~CHRIST, HAVE MERCY ON US. |
| Living bread that came down from heaven, | ~CHRIST, HAVE MERCY ON US. |
| Bread of Life for a hungry world, | ~CHRIST, HAVE MERCY ON US. |
| Chalice of blessing, | ~CHRIST, HAVE MERCY ON US. |
| Precious Blood that washes away our sins, | ~CHRIST, HAVE MERCY ON US. |
| Memorial of God's undying love, | ~CHRIST, HAVE MERCY ON US. |
| Food that lasts for eternal life, | ~CHRIST, HAVE MERCY ON US. |
| Mystery of faith, | ~CHRIST, HAVE MERCY ON US. |
| Medicine of immortality, | ~CHRIST, HAVE MERCY ON US. |
| Food of God's chosen, | ~CHRIST, HAVE MERCY ON US. |
| Perpetual presence in our tabernacles, | ~CHRIST, HAVE MERCY ON US. |

Viaticum of those who die
in the Lord, ~CHRIST, HAVE MERCY ON US.
Pledge of future glory, ~CHRIST, HAVE MERCY ON US.

Be merciful, ~SPARE US, GOOD LORD.
Be merciful, ~GRACIOUSLY HEAR US, GOOD LORD.

By the great longing you had to eat
the Passover with your
disciples, ~GOOD LORD, DELIVER US.
By your humility in washing
their feet, ~GOOD LORD, DELIVER US.
By your loving gift of this
divine sacrament, ~GOOD LORD, DELIVER US.
By the five wounds of your
precious body, ~GOOD LORD, DELIVER US.
By your sacrificial death on
the cross, ~GOOD LORD, DELIVER US.
By the piercing of your sacred
heart, ~GOOD LORD, DELIVER US.
By your rising to new life, ~GOOD LORD, DELIVER US.
By your gift of the Paraclete
Spirit, ~GOOD LORD, DELIVER US.
By your return in glory to
judge the living and the
dead, ~GOOD LORD, DELIVER US.

Lamb of God, you take away
the sins of the world, ~HAVE MERCY ON US.
Lamb of God, you take away
the sins of the world, ~HAVE MERCY ON US.
Lamb of God, you take away
the sins of the world, ~HAVE MERCY ON US.

You gave them bread from heaven to be their food.
~AND THIS BREAD CONTAINED ALL GOODNESS.

Let us pray.

Lord Jesus Christ,
you gave us the Eucharist
as the memorial of your suffering and death.
May our worship of this sacrament of your body
    and blood
help us to experience the salvation you won for us
and the peace of your kingdom,
where you live with the Father and the Holy Spirit,
one God for ever and ever.
~AMEN.[93]

## *Litany of Loreto*

| | |
|---|---|
| Lord, have mercy. | ~LORD, HAVE MERCY. |
| Christ, have mercy. | ~CHRIST, HAVE MERCY. |
| Lord, have mercy. | ~LORD, HAVE MERCY. |
| God our Father in heaven, | ~HAVE MERCY ON US. |
| God the Son, Redeemer of the world, | ~HAVE MERCY ON US. |
| God the Holy Spirit, | ~HAVE MERCY ON US. |
| Holy Trinity, one God, | ~HAVE MERCY ON US. |
| Holy Mary, | ~PRAY FOR US. |
| Holy mother of God, | ~PRAY FOR US. |
| Most honored of virgins, | ~PRAY FOR US. |
| Mother of Christ, | ~PRAY FOR US. |
| Mother of the church, | ~PRAY FOR US. |
| Mother of divine grace, | ~PRAY FOR US. |
| Mother most pure, | ~PRAY FOR US. |
| Mother of chaste love, | ~PRAY FOR US. |
| Mother and virgin, | ~PRAY FOR US. |
| Sinless Mother, | ~PRAY FOR US. |
| Dearest of mothers, | ~PRAY FOR US. |

| | |
|---|---|
| Model of motherhood, | ~PRAY FOR US. |
| Mother of good counsel, | ~PRAY FOR US. |
| Mother of our Creator, | ~PRAY FOR US. |
| Mother of our Savior, | ~PRAY FOR US. |
| | |
| Virgin most wise, | ~PRAY FOR US. |
| Virgin rightly praised, | ~PRAY FOR US. |
| Virgin rightly renowned, | ~PRAY FOR US. |
| Virgin most powerful, | ~PRAY FOR US. |
| Virgin gentle in mercy, | ~PRAY FOR US. |
| Faithful virgin, | ~PRAY FOR US. |
| Mirror of justice, | ~PRAY FOR US. |
| Throne of wisdom, | ~PRAY FOR US. |
| Cause of our joy, | ~PRAY FOR US. |
| | |
| Shrine of the Spirit, | ~PRAY FOR US. |
| Glory of Israel, | ~PRAY FOR US. |
| Vessel of selfless devotion, | ~PRAY FOR US. |
| Mystical rose, | ~PRAY FOR US. |
| Tower of David, | ~PRAY FOR US. |
| Tower of ivory, | ~PRAY FOR US. |
| House of gold, | ~PRAY FOR US. |
| Ark of the covenant, | ~PRAY FOR US. |
| Gate of heaven, | ~PRAY FOR US. |
| Morning Star, | ~PRAY FOR US. |
| Health of the sick, | ~PRAY FOR US. |
| Refuge of sinners, | ~PRAY FOR US. |
| Comfort of the troubled, | ~PRAY FOR US. |
| Help of Christians, | ~PRAY FOR US. |
| | |
| Queen of angels, | ~PRAY FOR US. |
| Queen of patriarchs and prophets, | ~PRAY FOR US. |
| Queen of apostles and martyrs, | ~PRAY FOR US. |
| Queen of confessors and virgins, | ~PRAY FOR US. |
| Queen of all saints, | ~PRAY FOR US. |
| Queen conceived in grace, | ~PRAY FOR US. |
| Queen raised up to glory, | ~PRAY FOR US. |

| Queen of the rosary, | ~PRAY FOR US. |
| Queen of the family, | ~PRAY FOR US. |
| Queen of peace, | ~PRAY FOR US. |

| Lamb of God, you take away the sins of the world, | ~HAVE MERCY ON US. |
| Lamb of God, you take away the sins of the world, | ~HAVE MERCY ON US. |
| Lamb of God, you take away the sins of the world, | ~HAVE MERCY ON US. |

| Pray for us, holy mother of God, | ~THAT WE MAY BECOME WORTHY OF THE PROMISES OF CHRIST. |

Let us pray:

Eternal God,
let your people enjoy constant health in mind and
body.
Through the intercession of the Virgin Mary
free us from the sorrows of this life
and lead us to happiness in the life to come.
Grant this through Christ our Lord.
~AMEN.[94]

### Litany of St. Joseph

| Lord, have mercy. | ~LORD, HAVE MERCY. |
| Christ, have mercy. | ~CHRIST, HAVE MERCY. |
| Lord, have mercy. | ~LORD, HAVE MERCY. |

| God our Father in heaven, | ~HAVE MERCY ON US. |
| God the Son, Redeemer of the world, | ~HAVE MERCY ON US. |
| God the Holy Spirit, | ~HAVE MERCY ON US. |

| | |
|---|---|
| Holy Trinity, one God, | ~HAVE MERCY ON US. |
| St. Joseph, | ~PRAY FOR US. |
| Noble son of the House of David, | ~PRAY FOR US. |
| Light of patriarchs, | ~PRAY FOR US. |
| Husband of the mother of God, | ~PRAY FOR US. |
| Guardian of the Virgin, | ~PRAY FOR US. |
| Foster father of the Son of God, | ~PRAY FOR US. |
| Faithful guardian of Christ, | ~PRAY FOR US. |
| Head of the holy family, | ~PRAY FOR US. |
| Joseph, chaste and just, | ~PRAY FOR US. |
| Joseph, prudent and brave, | ~PRAY FOR US. |
| Joseph, obedient and loyal, | ~PRAY FOR US. |
| Pattern of patience, | ~PRAY FOR US. |
| Lover of poverty, | ~PRAY FOR US. |
| Model of workers, | ~PRAY FOR US. |
| Example to parents, | ~PRAY FOR US. |
| Guardian of virgins, | ~PRAY FOR US. |
| Pillar of family life, | ~PRAY FOR US. |
| Comfort of the troubled, | ~PRAY FOR US. |
| Hope of the sick, | ~PRAY FOR US. |
| Patron of the dying, | ~PRAY FOR US. |
| Terror of evil spirits, | ~PRAY FOR US. |
| Protector of the church, | ~PRAY FOR US. |
| Lamb of God, you take away the sins of the world, | ~HAVE MERCY ON US. |
| Lamb of God, you take away the sins of the world, | ~HAVE MERCY ON US. |
| Lamb of God, you take away the sins of the world, | ~HAVE MERCY ON US. |
| God made him master of his household, | ~AND PUT HIM IN CHARGE OF ALL THAT HE OWNED. |

Let us pray:

Almighty God,
in your infinite wisdom and love
you chose Joseph to be the husband of Mary,
the mother of your Son.
As we enjoy his protection on earth
may we have the help of his prayers in heaven.
We ask this through Christ our Lord.
~AMEN.[95]

### Litany of the Seven Gifts of the Spirit

Come, Spirit of Wisdom, and give us a taste
   for things divine:
~COME, HOLY SPIRIT!

Come, Spirit of Understanding, and show us
     everything in the light of eternity:
~COME, HOLY SPIRIT!

Come, Spirit of Counsel, and direct our hearts
     and minds toward our heavenly home:
~COME, HOLY SPIRIT!

Come, Spirit of Might, and strengthen us
   against every evil inclination:
~COME, HOLY SPIRIT!

Come, Spirit of Knowledge, and lift our hearts on
     high:
~COME, HOLY SPIRIT!

Come, Spirit of Godliness, and fill us with the love
     of God and our neighbor:
~COME, HOLY SPIRIT!

Come, Spirit of Awe before the majesty of God,
and make us tremble with respect and
reverence before the Holy and Undivided
Trinity:
~COME, HOLY SPIRIT!

When you send forth your Spirit they are created
~AND YOU RENEW THE FACE OF THE EARTH.

Let us pray:

Holy Spirit of God,
final gift of our blessed Savior
as he ascended into heaven:
Pour out the seven gifts on your church,
renew and refresh it for service,
and inspire each one of us anew
as we walk with Jesus
under the mighty hand of God.
Blessed be God, now and for ever!
~AMEN.

Glory to the Father, and to the Son, and to the
Holy Spirit:
as it was in the beginning, is now, and will be for
ever. Amen.

## Litany of the Beatitudes

We are all looking for happiness in this world and in the
next. Jesus, God's Word to us and to all humanity, is
our teacher and guide on this quest, and the Sermon
on the Mount contains his finest and most accessible
teaching (Matthew 5—7). This peerless sermon opens

with the Beatitudes, which contradict the cultural values of Jesus' day by asserting that only those who are poor, mournful, meek, hungry for holiness, merciful, clean of heart, peacemakers, and persecuted are blessed in God's sight, fulfill the law of love, fear no condemnation, and are genuine Christians.

Blessed are the poor in spirit,
for theirs is the kingdom of heaven.
Blessed are they who mourn
for they will be comforted.
Blessed are the meek,
for they will inherit the land.
Blessed are they who hunger and thirst
    for righteousness,
for they will be satisfied.
Blessed are the merciful,
for they will be shown mercy.
Blessed are the clean of heart,
for they will see God.
Blessed are the peacemakers,
for they will be called children of God.
Blessed are they who are persecuted
    for the sake of righteousness,
for theirs is the kingdom of heaven.

Matthew 5:3–10, NAB

The Beatitudes are like rungs on a ladder, which Christ has arranged in an exact order. There is a pattern in his arrangement. Each step builds on

the foundation of the previous step, each leads
to the next, and each is indispensable. We can't
divide them up, retaining those we find appealing
and leaving those we don't care for to others, as if
one could specialize: "I'll take peacemaking, you
can have purity of heart."

Jim Forest[96]

## 1. Blessed are the poor in spirit.

Blessed are the poor, the humiliated, the
powerless, the trampled upon, those without
recourse to law or to human pity; those who prefer
poverty to riches, want rather than luxury, penury
rather than wealth; those who do not boast of
their intelligence or education or privileged place
in society.

## 2. Blessed are they who mourn.

Blessed are they who suffer illness and disease,
death of the body and death of the spirit; who
suffer from injustice and exploitation; who live
without beauty, without music, without friendship.

## 3. Blessed are the meek.

Blessed are they who suffer from the rich and the
proud in patience, gentleness, and humility.

## 4. Blessed are they who hunger and thirst for righteousness.

Blessed are they who long to become holy in the
pattern of Christ Jesus, who long to walk in his

footsteps, to understand his gospel better and better, and to imitate his saints.

## 5. Blessed are the merciful.
Blessed are they who set aside justice in favor of mercy; who fully recognize that we are completely dependent on the mercy of God ourselves and not on the rigors of divine justice; those who listen to their hearts rather than to their sense of justice; who prefer to forgive rather than punish; who shudder at the presumption of mercilessness; who cannot abide the torture of other human beings, no matter how bad.

## 6. Blessed are the clean of heart.
Blessed are they who know that if the eye is sound the whole body will be filled with light (Matthew 6:22–23); that if we diligently cleanse ourselves of sin we will more clearly see the will of God; that if we avoid the filthiness of rash judgment, we ourselves will not be judged harshly; that if we are chaste we shall learn how to love.

## 7. Blessed are the peacemakers.
Blessed are they who understand that Jesus is the Prince of Peace and who work with might and main to keep peace in their families, their neighborhood, their city, their country, and in the world.

## 8. Blessed are they who are persecuted for the sake of righteousness.

Blessed are they who cling to the Law of the Gospel in spite of all that the world, the flesh, and the devil can do; who bless their persecutors, those who malign them, falsely depict them, maliciously lie about them; those who meekly, patiently, and with humility think well of those who persecute them and honestly thank them in their hearts for this great and finest blessing.

### LITANY OF THE BEATITUDES

Lord Jesus, teacher of righteousness;
~GIVE US TRUE HAPPINESS AND EVERY BLESSING.

Bless the poor and humble in spirit;
~MAKE THEM INHERIT THE KINGDOM OF HEAVEN.

Bless those who mourn for lost blessings;
~BE THEIR COMFORT IN TIME OF TROUBLE.

Bless those who are meek and humble of heart;
~LET THEM INHERIT WHAT GOD HAS PROMISED.

Bless those who hunger and thirst for what God
    requires;
~AND FILL THEM WITH DIVINE WHOLENESS.

Bless those who are merciful toward others;
~MAY GOD BE MERCIFUL TO THEM IN TURN.

Bless those who are pure in heart;
~LET THEM SEE GOD IN THE LIGHT OF GLORY.

Bless those who make peace on earth;
~AND CALL THEM THE CHILDREN OF GOD.

Bless those who are persecuted for being holy;
~GIVE THEM POSSESSION OF THE KINGDOM OF
GOD.

Bless those who are slandered and insulted for
your sake;
~MAKE THEM HAPPY AND GLAD
FOR THEIR REWARD IS GREAT IN THEIR
HEAVENLY HOME.

Pause for special intentions.

**PRAYER**
Lord Jesus, light of the world,
you taught us how to be happy
in this life and in the next,
by walking in your blessed footsteps:
Make us humble, pure and merciful;
help us to make peace and pursue holiness,
and to rejoice when we are persecuted,
slandered, and insulted for your sake.
Illumine our hearts with your sacred teaching,
O Savior of the world,
and form us as your devout disciples
and the children of God your Father,
to the glory of your holy Name.
~AMEN.

## HYMN

Christ is the world's Redeemer,
The lover of the pure,
The fount of heavenly wisdom,
Our trust and hope secure;
The armor of his soldiers,
The Lord of earth and sky;
Our health while we are living,
Our life when we shall die.

St. Columba of Iona (521–597)

## AN INCANTATION

God with me lying down,
God with me rising up,
God with me in each ray of light,
Not a ray of joy without him,
  Not one ray without him.

Christ with me sleeping,
Christ with me waking,
Christ with me watching,
Every day and night,
  Each day and night.

God with me protecting,
The Lord with me directing,
The Spirit with me strengthening,
For ever and for evermore,
  For ever and for evermore. Amen.

Alexander Carmichael[97]

# V
# *Sacraments*

## A Preparation for Holy Communion in the Home

Those who are homebound, either permanently or temporarily, may arrange for a eucharistic minister (priest, deacon, or other designated person) to bring them Holy Communion so that they may share in the celebration of the eucharistic community. The prayers below are meant to prepare communicants to receive communion devoutly before the eucharistic minister arrives at the home, hospital, nursing home, or hospice. They may be led by any family member or friend. In the sick person's room, it is customary to prepare a table with a crucifix, candles, and a clean white cloth for the convenience of the eucharistic minister.

**ONE:** In the name of the Father, † and of the Son, and of the Holy Spirit.

**ALL:** ~AMEN.

**HYMN**
The strife is o'er, the battle done,
The victory of life is won;
The song of triumph has begun.
Alleluia!

The powers of death have done their worst,
But Christ their legion has dispersed:
Let shouts of holy joy outburst.
Alleluia!

The three sad days are quickly sped,
Christ rises glorious from the dead:
All glory to our risen Head!
Alleluia!

Lord, by your wounds on Calvary
From death's dread sting your servants free,
That we may live eternally.
Alleluia![98]

## PSALM 117: A UNIVERSAL HYMN OF PRAISE

ANTIPHON Holy is God, HOLY AND STRONG,
HOLY AND LIVING FOR EVER!

Praise the LORD, all you nations!
Give glory, all you peoples!
~HOLY IS GOD, HOLY AND STRONG, HOLY AND
   LIVING FOR EVER!

The LORD's love for us is strong;
The LORD is faithful for ever.
~HOLY IS GOD, HOLY AND STRONG, HOLY AND
   LIVING FOR EVER!

Glory to the Father, and to the Son, and to the
   Holy Spirit:
~HOLY IS GOD, HOLY AND STRONG, HOLY AND
   LIVING FOR EVER!

As it was in the beginning, is now, and will be for
ever. Amen.

~HOLY IS GOD, HOLY AND STRONG, HOLY AND
LIVING FOR EVER!

## PSALM PRAYER
**ONE:** Let us pray (pause for silent prayer):

Holy, mighty, and immortal God,
glorified by the cherubim,
worshipped by the seraphim,
and adored by all the powers of heaven:
You created us in your own image
and restored and adorned us with every good gift
in Jesus Messiah, our Lord and Savior.
Be pleased to accept our hymns of praise,
sanctify our souls and bodies,
and forgive us our transgressions;
for you are holy, O God, and we glorify you,
Father, Son, and Holy Spirit,
now and always, and for ever and ever.
**ALL:** ~AMEN.

## A READING FROM THE HOLY GOSPEL ACCORDING TO JOHN 6:27, 32–33
Jesus said to the crowds, "Do not work for the
food that perishes, but for the food that endures
for eternal life, which the Son of Man will give
you. For it is on him that God the Father has set
his seal. Very truly, I tell you, it was not Moses

who gave you the bread from heaven, but it is my
Father who gives you the true bread from heaven.
For the bread of God is that which comes down
from heaven and gives life to the world."

**SILENT PRAYER**

**RESPONSE**
My flesh is true food, alleluia!
~AND MY BLOOD IS TRUE DRINK, ALLELUIA!

**THE LORD'S PRAYER**
**ONE:** Let us pray as Jesus taught us:
**ALL:** ~Our Father in heaven,
hallowed be your name,
your kingdom come,
your will be done,
on earth as in heaven.
Give us today our daily bread.
Forgive us our sins
as we forgive those who sin against us.
Save us from the time of trial
and deliver us from evil.
For the kingdom, the power, and the glory are
      yours
now and for ever. Amen.

Lord Jesus Christ,
you gave us the Eucharist
as the memorial of your suffering and death.
May our worship of this sacrament
   of your body and blood
help us to experience the salvation
   you won for us
and the peace of the kingdom
where you live with the Father and the Holy Spirit,
one God, for ever and ever.
~AMEN.[99]

Blessed be Jesus in the most holy Sacrament of the
      Altar.
~AMEN.

# A Preparation for the
# Sacrament of Anointing

In time of serious sickness we remember that Jesus himself instituted for us a special sacrament of healing and consolation. Here is a form of private preparation for those who are sick, and for their family and friends who watch over them. Solidarity around a sickbed is a true sign of Christian love and concern.

**ONE:** Our help ✝ is in the name of the Lord,
**ALL:** ~WHO MADE HEAVEN AND EARTH.

### HYMN

Alone, in depths of woe,
Upon that scornful tree
Hangs Christ, redeemer of the world,
In shame and agony.

His feet and hands outstretched
By hammered nails are torn;
In mocking, on his head is thrust
A crown of bitter thorn.

Come, kneel before the Lord:
He shed for us his blood;
He died the victim of pure love
To make us one with God.[100]

### A READING FROM THE EPISTLE OF ST. JAMES 5:13–16

Are any among you suffering? They should pray. Are any cheerful? They should sing songs of praise. Are any among you sick? They should call for the elders of the church and have them pray over them, anointing them with oil in the name of the Lord. The prayer of faith will save the sick, and the Lord will raise them up; and anyone who has committed sins will be forgiven. Therefore confess your sins to one another, and pray for one another, so that you may be healed. The prayer of the righteous is powerful and effective.

**ONE:** The Word of the Lord.
**ALL:** THANKS BE TO GOD.

## A READING FROM THE HOLY GOSPEL ACCORDING TO ST. MARK 6:7, 12–13

Jesus called the twelve and began to send them out two by two, and gave them authority over the unclean spirits. . . . So they went out and proclaimed that all should repent. They cast out many demons, and anointed with oil many who were sick and cured them.

**ALL:** PRAISE TO YOU, LORD JESUS CHRIST.

### PRAYER
**ONE:** Let us pray in silence for the sick:

Lord Jesus Christ, healer of our souls and bodies, during your life on earth you went about doing
   good,
healing every manner of sickness and disease, strengthening, curing, comforting, and consoling.

You sent out your holy apostles with authority
to preach repentance, to cast out unclean spirits,
and to anoint the sick with oil for their recovery.
In obedience to your command, O gracious Lord,
we pray over these persons, and lay hands on
     them,
in preparation for the sacrament of anointing.
May the prayer of faith save the sick,
drive away all pain from their souls and bodies,
forgive all their sins,
and raise them up to serve you cheerfully
for the rest of their life.

**ALL:** BLESSED BE JESUS, FRIEND OF THE HUMAN
     RACE!

**THE LORD'S PRAYER**
**ONE:** Let us pray as Jesus taught us:
**ALL:** ~Our Father in heaven,
hallowed be your name,
your kingdom come,
your will be done,
on earth as in heaven.
Give us today our daily bread.
Forgive us our sins
as we forgive those who sin against us.
Save us from the time of trial
and deliver us from evil.
For the kingdom, the power, and the glory are
     yours
now and for ever. Amen.

## CLOSING PRAYER

**ONE:** Almighty and everlasting God,
by the mission of your divine Son
you bring health and healing to the whole world.
We praise and thank you for the gift of health
and pray that it may be restored to Name,
so that he/she may serve you worthily
all the remaining days of her/his life.
Blessed be the Holy and Undivided Trinity,
now and always and for ever and ever.
**ALL:** ~AMEN.

## A FINAL BLESSING (NUMBERS 6:24–26)

**ONE:** May the Lord bless us and keep us;
May the Lord make his face to shine upon us,
and be gracious to us;
May the Lord lift up his countenance upon us,
and † give us peace.
**ALL:** ~AMEN.

# Notes

1. Thomas à Kempis (1380-1471), *The Imitation of Christ*, ed. Harold C. Gardiner (Garden City, NY: Image Books, 1963), 94.

2. Sacred Heart of Jesus, Roman Missal.

3. St. Francis of Assisi (1181–1226), "A Letter to the General Chapter of the Order," ed. Marion A. Habig, *Writings and Early Biographies of St. Francis*, 4th revised edition (Chicago, IL: Franciscan Herald Press, 1983), 108.

4. After St. Ignatius of Antioch (+ ca, 107), Letter to the Church at Smyrna 1; trans. W.A. Jurgens, *The Faith of the Early Fathers* (Collegeville, MN: The Liturgical Press, 1970), I, 24.

5. Julian of Norwich (1343–ca. 1423), *Showings*, chap. 15 (short text), trans. Edmund Colledge and James Walsh (New York: Paulist Press, 1978), 151, 152.

6. Attributed to St. Patrick (389–461) but actually composed in Latin a little later; translated by William G. Storey.

7. Mother Teresa of Calcutta (1910–1997), *A Simple Path* (New York: Ballantine Books, 1995), 13.

8. Gail Ramshaw-Schmidt, "Naming the Trinity: Orthodoxy and Inclusivity," *Worship* 60, no. 6 (November 1986): 497–498.

9. *A Simple Path*, xxxiii.

10. Alexander Carmichael, *Celtic Invocations* (Noroton, CT: Vineyard Books, 1977), 41.

11. *Phos hilaron*, late second century, translated from the Greek by William G. Storey.

12. *The Book of Common Prayer* (New York: Seabury Press, 1979).

13. William Barclay (1907–1978), *Prayers for Help and Healing* (Harper and Row, 1968).
14. Alexander Carmichael, *Celtic Invocations* (Noroton, CT: Vineyard Books, 1972), 121.
15. Teresa of Ávila (1515–1582), *The Collected Works of Teresa of Avila*, volume 3, trans. Kieran Kavanaugh and Otilio Rodriguez. Used by permission of ICS Publications, Washington, DC, and the Washington Province of the Discalced Carmelites.
16. John A. Hardon, S.J., of the Detroit Province of the Society of Jesus.
17. Attributed to St. Francis of Assisi (1181–1226) but actually by a Norman priest in a French periodical, *La Clochette*, no. 12, December 1912, 285.
18. St. Bernard of Clairvaux (1091–1153), translated by Ray Palmer (1808–1887).
20. Tridentine Missal, Feast of the Holy Name.
21. St. Bernard of Clairvaux (1090–1153), *Sermon 15 on the Canticle of Canticles*, translated by William G. Storey.
22. See also G.E.H. Palmer, Philip Sherrard, Kallistos Ware, *The Philokalia* (London: Faber and Faber, 1979). The Philokalia is a collection of texts on prayer and the spiritual life written between the fourteenth and fifteenth centuries by spiritual masters of the Orthodox tradition. See also *The Way of the Pilgrim*, trans. R.M. French (New York: Harper and Brothers, 1952); Lev Gillet, *The Jesus Prayer*, ed. Kallistos Ware (Crestwood, NY: St. Vladimir's Seminary Press, 1987) and a new critical edition by Aleksei Pentkovsky (New York: Paulist Press, 1999).
23. St. John of Damascus (676–760) from *Voices in the Wilderness: An Anthology of Patristic Prayers*, ed. and trans. Nikolaos S. Hatzinikolaou (Brookline, MA: Holy Cross Orthodox Press, 1988).
24. St. Francis of Assisi (1181–1226), "A Letter to the Entire Order," in *Writings and Early Biographies*,

ed. Marion A. Habig (Quincy, IL: Franciscan Herald Press, 1983), 105–06.

25. *Anima Christi*, early fourteenth century, translated by William G. Storey.

26. Pope John XXlll (1881–1963) from Michael Buckley, *The Catholic Prayer Book,* Servant Books, 1984. Used with permission of St. Anthony Messenger Press.

27. St. Thomas More (1478–1535), English martyr, from Michael Buckley, *The Catholic Prayer Book,* Servant Books, 1984. Used with permission of St. Anthony Messenger Press.

28. Mother Teresa, *A Simple Path* (New York: Ballantine Books, 1995), 37–38.

29. James Quinn, *Praise for All Seasons* (Pittsburgh: Selah, 1994), 66.

30. Roman Liturgy, Good Friday.

31. St. Thomas Aquinas, OP (1225–1274), "De passione Christi," *Summa Theologiae* III, 46, 5, (London: Dominican Fathers, 1921), alt. by William G. Storey.

32. Julian of Norwich (1343–ca. 1423), *Showings*, chap. 10 (short text), trans. Edmund Colledge and James Walsh (New York: Paulist Press, 1978), 141–42.

33. John Rippon, *A Selection of Hymns* (Chillicothe: J. Hellings, 1815), # 477, alt. by William G. Storey.

34. St. Angela of Foligno (1248–1309), "The Divine Consolation," in Paul de Jaegher, *Christian Mystics of the Middle Ages* (New York: Dover, 2004), 42–43.

35. English Prymer, fifteenth century, translated by William G. Storey.

36. Julian of Norwich (1343–ca. 1423), *Showings*, chap. 4 (short text), trans. Edmund Colledge and James Walsh (New York: Paulist Press, 1978), 131.

37. From a devotion to the Virgin Mary, translated and altered by William G. Storey.

38. *Marialis Cultus* (Feb. 2, 1974), 15, 13.

39. *A Book of Prayers* (Washington, DC: ICEL, 1982), 35.

40. *Ave, Maris Stella*, ninth century, translated from the Latin by Frank Quinn, OP.

41. Latin antiphon, eleventh century, from *A Book of Prayers* (Washington, DC: ICEL, 1982), #24, 34.

42. Translated from several Latin texts of the twelfth and thirteenth centuries by William G. Storey.

43. St. Francis of Assisi (1181–1226), *Writings and Early Biographies*, ed. Marion A. Habig (Quincy, IL: Franciscan Herald Press, 1983), 135–36.

44. A sixteenth-century abridgment of a fifteenth-century prayer, much popularized by Père Claude Bernard (1588–1641), from *A Book of Prayers* (Washington, DC: ICEL, 1982), 34.

45. Anonymous, fourteenth-century, translated from the Middle English by Dolores Warwick Frese, professor of English, the University of Notre Dame. Used with permission.

46. St. Francis of Assisi (1181–1226), "The Office of the Passion," in *Writings and Early Biographies*, ed. Marion A. Habig (Quincy, IL: Franciscan Herald Press, 1983), 142.

47. Thomas McNally and William G. Storey, eds., *Day by Day: The Notre Dame Prayerbook for Students* (Notre Dame, IN: Ave Maria Press, 2004), 32.

48. William G. Storey, *Mother of the Americas* (Chicago: LTP, 2003), 66.

49. By permission of Madonna House Apostolate, Combermere, Ontario.

50. Adapted from liturgical prayers attributed to Bishop Serapion of Thmuis (Egypt, + after 362); Lucien Deiss, C.S.Sp., *Springtime of the Liturgy* (Collegeville, MN: The Liturgical Press, 1967), 189.

51. St. Philip Howard (1557–1595) from Michael Buckley, *The Catholic Prayer Book*, Servant Books, 1984. Used with permission of St. Anthony Messenger Press.

52. *Ave, verum corpus*, Roman liturgy.

53. St. Macrina (326–380), from *Early Christian Prayers*, ed. A. Hamman and trans. Walter Mitchell (London: Longmans, 1961). Reprinted by permission of Pearson Education Ltd.

54. Adapted from the Tridentine Liturgy of the Dying.

55. Adapted from the old Roman Ritual.

56. The old Roman Ritual.

57. Thomas à Kempis (1380–1471), *The Imitation of Christ*, ed. Harold C. Gardiner (Garden City, NY: Image Books, 1963), 94.

58. *Dies irae*, thirteenth century, translated by Sir Walter Scott.

59. John L. Bell and Graham Maule © 1996, Iona Community. GIA Publ. Inc., distributor in North America, 7404 South Mason Ave. Chicago, IL 60638.

60. All Souls, Roman Missal, #1.

61. Church of the Province of New Zealand, *The New Zealand Prayer Book* (Auckland, NZ: William Collins, 1989), 856, #5.

62. Ibid., 860.

63. Elsie Maclay, *Green Winter: Celebrations of Later Life* (New York: Henry Holt and Co., 1977), 61.

64. Pseudo-Dionysius, Mystical Theology I, 1 from *The Classics of Western Spirituality*, trans. from the Greek by Colm Luibheid. (New York/Mahwah, NJ: Paulist Press, 1987), 135.

65. Community of St. Mary the Virgin, Wantage.

66. James Quinn, SJ, *Praise for All Seasons* (Pittsburgh: Selah, 1994), 68.

67. Joseph Mary Plunkett (1887–1916), (Dublin: The Talbot Press, 1916), 50.

68. Anonymous, sixteenth century, translated from the Spanish by Sister M. Katharine Elaine, in *The Tree and the Master*, ed. Sr. Mary Immaculate (New York: Random House, 1965).

69. St. Francis of Assisi (1181–1226), *Writings and Early Biographies*, ed. Marion A. Habig (Quincy, IL: Franciscan Herald Press, 1983), 86.

70. John L. Bell, Iona Community; distributed by GIA, Chicago, Il.

71. St. Thomas More (1478–1535), English martyr. From *The Wisdom and Wit of Blessed Thomas More*,

ed. T. E. Bridgett (New York: Catholic Publication Society, 1892).

72. Lancelot Andrewes (1556–1626), *Preces Privatae*, translated by William G. Storey.

73. *The Book of Common Prayer* (New York: Seabury Press, 1979), 125.

74. *The Order of Evening Worship in the Meeting House on Star Island* (Boston: The Merrymount Press, 1903), altered by William G. Storey.

75. Alexander Carmichael, *Celtic Invocations* (Noroton, CT: Vineyard Books, 1972), 73.

76. Sarum Prymer, 1527, translated by William G. Storey.

77. *Te Deum laudamus*, translated by C. A. Walworth (1835).

78. *Veni, Creator Spiritus*, attributed to Rabanus Maurus (780–856), translated by John Dryden (1631–1701).

79. Adapted by Charles F. Whiston from an ancient prayer in Elizabeth Goudge, *A Diary of Prayer* (New York: Coward-McCann, 1966), 93.

80. Tom Noe in *Day by Day: The Notre Dame Prayer Book for Students*, eds. Thomas McNally and William G. Storey (Notre Dame, IN: Ave Maria Press, 2004), 91.

81. St. Francis of Assisi (1181–1226), translated by William G. Storey.

82. St. Francis of Assisi (1181–1226), *Writings and Early Biographies*, ed. Marion A. Habig (Quincy, IL: Franciscan Herald Press, 1983), 124–26.

83. After St. Gregory the Great, Homily 29; *Breviarium Romanum*, Feria V in Octava Ascensionis; translated by William G. Storey.

84. Trinity Sunday, Roman Missal.

85. Byzantine Liturgy, translated by William G. Storey.

86. Feast of the Sacred Heart, Roman Missal.

87. This prayer has been in the Roman Missal since 1570. *A Book of Prayers* (Washington, DC: ICEL, 1982), 6, #5.

88. St. Catherine of Siena, *The Life and Sayings of St. Catherine of Siena (1347–1380)*, trans. Paul Garvin. (Staten Island, NY: Alba House, 1964).

89. Edward Perronet (1724–1792); alt. by John Rippon (1751–1836); alt. by William G. Storey, 2006.

90. Approved by Pope Leo XIII (1810–1903) for use throughout the world. *Book of Prayers* (Washington, DC: ICEL, 1982), 21–23.

91. Many of the invocations in this litany can be traced to the seventeenth century. Approved by Pope Leo XIII (1810–1903). *A Book of Prayers* (Washington, DC: ICEL, 1982), 24–25.

92. Joseph Raya and Jose de Vinck, eds. and trans., *Byzantine Daily Worship* (Allendale, NJ: Alleluia Press, 1969), 989–90.

93. Most of the invocations in this litany are drawn from popular prayer books of the nineteenth and twentieth centuries.

94. A Marian litany containing some of these invocations was in use in the twelfth century. It was recorded in its present form (apart from a few additions by recent popes) at Loreto in 1558 and approved by Sixtus V (1521–1590). *Book of Prayers* (Washington, DC: ICEL, 1982), 28–29.

95. Approved by Pope Pius X (1835–1914). *Book of Prayers* (Washington, DC: ICEL, 1982), 30–31.

96. Jim Forest, *The Ladder of the Beatitudes* (Maryknoll, NY: Orbis Books, 1999), 2.

97. Alexander Carmichael, *Celtic Invocations* (Noroton, CT: Vineyard Books, 1972), 55.

98. Translated by Francis Potts, 1861.

99. Corpus Christi, Roman Missal.

100. Text adapted by Edward Caswall (1814–1878) from *Saevo dolorum turbine*, Roman Breviary, (Bologna, 1827).

# Acknowledgments

The Litany of the Holy Name of Jesus, the Litany of the Sacred Heart, the Litany of Loreto, the Litany of St. Joseph, the Sub tuum praesidium, the Salve Regina, and the Memorare are taken from *A Book of Prayers 1982*, International Committee on English in the Liturgy, Inc. (ICEL); four opening prayers from the Roman Missal, copyright © 1973 by ICEL. All rights reserved.

An excerpt from *Pseudo-Dionysius: The Complete Works*, translated by Colm Luibheid. Copyright © Paulist Press, Inc., New York/Mahwah, NJ. Reprinted by permission of Paulist Press, Inc. www.paulistpress.com

Excerpts from Julian of Norwich, *Showings*, translated by Edmund Colledge, OSA and James Walsh, SJ. Copyright © 1978 by Paulist Press, Inc., New York/Mahwah, NJ. Reprinted by permission of Paulist Press, Inc. www.paulistpress.com

Three items by Mother Teresa of Calcutta from *A Simple Path*, edited by Lucinda Vardey, copyright © 1995 by Lucinda Vardey. Used by pernmission of Ballantine Books, a division of Random House, Inc.

An anonymous poem from Sr. Katharine, CSC, *The Tree and the Master*. © Random House 1965.

Two excerpts from Thomas à Kempis, *The Imitation of Christ*, edited by Harold C. Gardiner, SJ Random Hours/Image Books, 1963.

Unless otherwise noted, all the Scripture quotations are taken from the New Revised Standard Version of the Bible © 1989, Division of Christian Education of the National Council of Churches of Christ in the USA and are used by permission. All rights reserved.

Scripture passages cited as "NAB" are taken from the *New American Bible with Revised New Testament and Psalms*, copyright © 1991, 1986, 1970 by the Confraternity of Christian Doctrine, Inc., Washington, DC. Used with permission. All rights reserved. No part of the *New American Bible* may be reproduced in any form without permission in writing from the copyright owner.

Scripture passages cited as "TEV" are taken from The Good News Bible, Today's English Version. New York: The American Bible Society, 1992.

Five passages from *A New Zealand Prayer Book He Karakia Mihinare ki o Aotearoa,* which is a publication of The Anglican Church in Aotearoa, New Zealand and Polynesia—Te Hahi Mihinare ki Aotearoa ki Niu Tireni, ki Nga Moutere o te Moana Nui a Kiwa, copyright © 1989 The Provincial Secretary, The Anglican Church in Aotearoa, New Zealand and Polynesia. PO Box 87188, Meadowbank, Aukland 1742, New Zealand.

Unless otherwise noted all the psalms are taken from *Psalms for Prayer and Worship: A Complete Liturgical Psalter* by John Holbert et al. Nashville: Abingdon Press, 1992.

Two hymns from James Quinn, SJ, *Prayer for All Seasons,* 1994. Used by permission of Selah Publishing Co., Inc. North American agent. www.selahpub.com. Used by permission.

The Gospel canticles of Mary, Zachary, and Simeon, the Te Deum, the Gloria in Excelsis, the Gloria Patri, and the Lord's Prayer are from *Praying Together: English Language Liturgical Consultation.* Nashville: Abingdon Press, 1988. ELLC.

A prayer of St. Macrina on Her Deathbed from A. Hamman, OFM, *Early Christian Prayers.* Longmans Green and Company, 1961. By permission of Pearson Education Ltd.

Three prayers taken from Michael Buckley, *The Catholic Prayer Book.* Copyright 1984. Published by Servant Books.

Used with permission of St. Anthony Messenger Press.
www.americancatholic.org

Two prayers from *The Book of Common Prayer 1979*. New
York: Church Publishing Inc.

One prayer from the *Collected Works of Teresa of Avila*,
volume 3. Used by permission of the Institute of Carmelite
Studies, Washington, DC.

"O God, before I sleep, from *Prayers for Help and Healing
by William Barclay*. Copyright © 1968 by William Barclay.
Reprinted by permission of HarperCollins Publishers.

One prayer of St. John of Damascus from *Voices in the
Wilderness*, 1988. By permission of Holy Cross Orthodox
Press.

A translation of an anonymous fourteenth century,
Middle English poet by Dolores Warwick Frese, Professor
of English, The University of Notre Dame. Used by
permission.

A translation of the Ave Maris Stella, "Praise to Mary,
heaven's gate," by Frank C. Quinn, OP. By permission of
the translator, the Aquinas Institute of Theology.

Two items from John L. Bell and Graham Maule, © 1996,
the Iona Community. Copyright © Wild Goose Resource
Group, Iona Community, Scotland, exclusive North
American Agent, 7404 S. Mason Ave., Chicago, IL 60638.
www.giamusic.com 800.442.1358 All rights reserved.
Used by permission.

The Litany of the Resurrection from *Byzantine Daily
Worship*, Alleluia Press, 1996. By permission.

A Novena Prayer by William G. Storey from *Mother
of the Americas: A Novena in Honor of Our Lady of
Guadalupe*, by William G. Storey © 2003 Archdiocese of
Chicago: Liturgy Training Publications www.Hp.org. All
rights reserved. Used with permission. Liturgy Training
Publications, 2003.

A paragraph from Jim Forest, *The Ladder of the Beatitudes*. Orbis Press, 1999. By permission.

A prayer of J. Robert Baker, professor of English, the University of West Virginia. By permision.

Two prayers by James M. Backes. By permission.

One prayer by Martha Carroll, minister, Southside Christian Church, South Bend, Indiana. By permission.

Two prayers by a priest of Holy Cross. Notre Dame, Indiana. By permission.

One prayer to Our Lady of Combermere by permission of Madonna House Publications, Combermere, Ontario. Canada.

Two prayers from *Day by Day: The Notre Dame Prayerbook for Students*. Ave Maria Press, 2004. By permission of Tom Noe and Ave Maria Press.

A version of the Lesser Doxology by Gail Ramshaw-Schmidt from Worship 60, 6 (November 1986). By permission of the Liturgical Press.

A prayer adapted from St. Ignatius of Antioch in W.A. Jurgens, The Faith of the Early Fathers, © 1970. By permission of The Liturgical Press

A prayer adapted from Bishop Serapion of Thmuis from Lucien Deiss, Springtime of the Liturgy, © 1967. By permission of the Liturgical Press.

A selection from the work: *Green Winter*, by Elise Maclay, Henry Holt, © d1990 Excerpted with permission of Sanford J. Greenburger Associates, Inc..

A prayer by John A. Hardon, SJ, "Jesus Help Me" by permission of the Detroit Province of the Society of Jesus.

Prayers without attribution can be considered to be composed or translated by the author.

# About the Author

William G. Storey is professor emeritus of Liturgy and Church History at the University of Notre Dame. He has compiled, edited, and authored some of the best-loved prayer books of our time, most notably *Lord, Hear Our Prayer; Hail Mary: A Marian Book of Hours; An Everyday Book of Hours; A Seasonal Book of Hours;* and *Mother of the Americas.* He resides in South Bend, Indiana.